W9-AOS-843

THE SOCIALLY RESPONSIBLE
GUIDE TO SMART INVESTING

THE SOCIALLY RESPONSIBLE GUIDE TO SMART INVESTING

IMPROVE YOUR PORTFOLIO AS YOU IMPROVE THE ENVIRONMENT

SAMUEL CASE

PRIMA PUBLISHING

Investment decisions have certain inherent risks. Prima therefore disclaims any warranties or representations, whether express or implied, concerning the accuracy or completeness of the information or advice contained in this book. Any investment a reader may make based on such information is at the reader's sole risk. You should carefully research or consult a qualified financial advisor before making any particular investment.

© 1996 by Samuel Case

All rights reserved. No part of this book may be reproduced or transmitted in any form or by any means, electronic or mechanical, including photocopying, recording, or by any information storage or retrieval system, without written permission from Prima Publishing, except for the inclusion of quotations in a review.

PRIMA PUBLISHING and colophon are trademarks of Prima Communications, Inc.

Library of Congress Cataloging-in-Publication Data

Case, Samuel.
The socially responsible guide to smart investing / Samuel Case.
    p. cm.
    Includes index.
    ISBN 0-7615-0328-5
    1. Investments—Environmental aspects.   2. Venture capital.
3. Technological innovations—Finance.   4. Social responsibility of
business.   5. New business enterprises—Finance.   I. Title.
HG4521.C287   1995
658.4'08—dc20   95-23779
                                                                        CIP

96 97 98 99 00 DD 10 9 8 7 6 5 4 3 2 1

Printed in the United States of America

How to Order:
Single copies may be ordered from Prima Publishing, P.O. Box 1260BK, Rocklin, CA 95677; telephone (916) 632-4400. Quantity discounts are also available. On your letterhead, include information concerning the intended use of the books and the number of books you wish to purchase.

CONTENTS

INTRODUCTION

The environmental movement is entering a new phase. Since Earth Day, 1970, environmentalists have been playing the role of biblical prophets, warning that the end of the world is at hand if we continue on our present course. They have been educating the public, prodding politicians, and railing against the anti-environmental practices of private industry.

As we will see in chapter 1, such activities have helped to bring about many positive changes. The environment is improving in numerous ways, but this very success has made the remaining problems seem less immediate to many people.

Other factors have also contributed to the public perception that the war for the environment is being won. The present administration, elected in 1992, appears friendly to the environment. Even large corporations seem to be thinking green, at least in their public pronouncements.

In spite of the real improvements, however, much of this perception of progress is mistaken. The administration has been able to make little headway in the face of opposition by special interest groups, and conservative factions are attempting to seriously weaken environmental laws. And, while some companies have altered their policies for the better, the Earth-friendly tone of present corporate ad campaigns obscures corporate opposition to any regulatory legislation or real change.

But while progress may be slow in government and corporate offices, advances in other areas are beginning to attract attention. Progress in environmentally friendly technology is beginning to upstage the political debate. Over the coming decades, we are going to see these new technologies replace the old and, in the process, make great changes in our world.

These innovative products and processes are going to succeed simply because they're *better*: they're cheaper, more effective, less polluting, and easier to employ. They are to the old technologies what the radio was to the telegraph, or the computer/word processor is to the typewriter.

Many of these new technologies are still in the research and development stage. The technologies we have lived with since the start of the Industrial Revolution have had many decades—in some cases, centuries—to optimize their efficiency. Years of concentrated research and development have raised such machines as the steam turbine and the internal combustion engine to high levels of performance. Most of the recent environmental technologies, on the other hand, measure their lives in one to three decades, some only in years.

But, as we will see in later chapters, despite this difference in age, the performance of the new methods is already beginning to match and, in some cases, surpass that of the old. For example, electricity from wind turbines and solar arrays is already beginning to compete in price with electricity generated by steam turbines run by fossil fuels. There are recycling systems currently in operation that turn organic waste into high-quality animal feed or fertilizer in 24 hours.

In short, it's becoming increasingly clear that much of the environmental future of the world will be decided in the research laboratories and the marketplace, not just in the halls of government. The financial bottom line is a very powerful persuader, one which even conservative politicians and giant corporations must observe.

This does not mean that government won't continue to play an important role. Voters still need to support environmental policies. For example, we need to support policies that make polluting industries pay the full costs to society of their production methods.

But some sustainable industries are already beginning to prove themselves more cost-effective than traditional ones. If we, in this country, do not support further development of these kinds of new technologies, we will find ourselves falling behind more progressive economies in Europe and Japan.

The American public remains strongly concerned about the environment. A recent poll found that 86 percent of Americans consider themselves "environmentalists." Ecologically sound products and services have already found many customers and will find millions more as their price and performance begin to match those of their older, less environmentally sound counterparts.

The change to environmentally friendly, sustainable technologies is a shift of historic magnitude. Over the coming decades, we will see our world transformed. This book describes the technologies that will affect this transformation and shows how you can help make it all happen.

Those with money to invest can become an integral part of this process. Investment capital is necessary to develop and market these new technologies, especially for small start-up companies. And in this exploding field, investors who choose wisely will see their capital grow as rapidly as these innovative companies.

THE SOCIALLY RESPONSIBLE GUIDE TO SMART INVESTING

CHAPTER 1

2050 C.E.*

Imagine, if you will, the world of 2050. The air is clear, the lakes and rivers run clean, the soil is rich. Wildlife thrives in the new growth of forests, in the air, and in the oceans. The human population has stabilized and hunger is a thing of the past. Everywhere, economies are thriving, even though most people are working shorter hours. Children learn about such things as war and street crime only in their history classes.

Most futurists and psychics are quick to point out that their predictions of the future are conditional. There are so many possible variables in any situation that all they, or anyone, can do is talk about trends and probabilities. But the only way to turn possibilities into reality is by having a vision and working toward it.

We need positive, joyful visions of the future. In the face of so many doomsday scenarios and visons of

*C.E.: Common Era

violent futures in the media, we must focus on what we want to happen. What we fear will happen is useful as a warning, but the kind of world portrayed on the previous page will come about only through holding the vision and working to make it happen.

But can we really succeed, or are the forces operating to degrade the environment too powerful? For an answer, in this chapter, we're first going to look at what we have accomplished in the last 25 years. After we view these few successes, however, we're going to have to talk about the dangerous environmental problems that remain unsolved.

How are we going to solve these and create a successful economy that harmonizes with the natural world? First, we need to see how the successes of the last two decades have come about. We have been doing some things right, and we'll take a close look at just what they are.

Realizing our vision of 2050, however, will require making changes of a more radical nature. Later in this chapter, we'll discuss some of the new ways of thinking that will lead us into a fresh new century.

FIRST, THE GOOD NEWS

Since 1970, the year of the first Earth Day, when concern for the environment began to operate as a powerful force for change, we have made tremendous progress. This progress has been much greater than most people dared to hope—and greater than most people realize.

Since the Clean Air Act was passed in 1970, the main components of smog have declined by about a third, even though there are 85 percent more vehicles on the road. Coal burning has doubled, but emissions of fine soot have fallen by 78 percent. As a result, the air in most cities is noticeably cleaner.

When the Clean Water Act went into effect in 1972, about two-thirds of the rivers, lakes, and bays in the United States were unsafe for swimming and fishing; today, two-thirds are safe. Better city sewage systems and improved treatment for industrial effluent have brought back many bodies of water from the brink of disaster.

The use of chlorofluorocarbons, which harm the ozone layer, is being phased out; there are now estimates that in about ten years, the ozone layer will begin to replenish itself. Toxic emissions of other chemicals are on a steep decline. Dioxin, for example, one of the most dangerous, is being replaced by safer compounds.

These successes have been echoed in other industrialized countries in Western Europe and in Japan, but they have not been well publicized. Perhaps this is because environmentalists are concerned that the public will assume our problems are being taken care of and grow complacent.

Political factions that advocate reducing the influence of government also have little interest in promoting these optimistic figures because they demonstrate that government regulations can often be effective. Indeed, environmental regulations have been such a success that those in Congress who oppose government regulations may have to make an exception for the environment, or face an angry electorate.

Reports of this progress need not downplay the amount of work yet to be done. Such reports indicate that much of what we are doing is successful—and that we need to continue. When we make a concerted effort to modify our habits and improve our technology, rapid and dramatic benefits ensue. Specifically, we need to resist all efforts—in Congress and elsewhere—to weaken the regulations that have brought us this far.

. . . NEXT, THE BAD NEWS

Despite the progress, there is a tremendous amount still to be done. Creating a clean environment and conserving natural resources are tasks that will require even more effort during the coming decades. While there has been progress in some areas such as those already mentioned, other areas, such as pollution of the soil and groundwater, have either not improved or have gotten worse.

Our health is seriously threatened by toxins in the environment. Various organochlorines, such as DDT, PCBs, and CFCs, are building up not just in the environment, but in our body fat. These poisonous chemicals are suspected of causing cancer, birth defects, and the declining sperm count in men. And these are only a few of the hazardous substances that continue to flow into the environment.

Particularly in the developing nations and the former communist countries, ecological degradation threatens the physical and financial health of billions of people. Devastation of the land and terrible pollution in the air and water coupled with exploding populations keep many of these countries in poverty.

Toxins from these countries also threaten our well-being. Fruits and vegetables are sprayed with pesticides such as DDT, which are outlawed in the U.S., then imported for our tables. Pollutants drift into the upper atmosphere or are carried around the world by wind and water. Radiation from the nuclear disaster at Chernobyl was blown into Western Europe by wind and rain. Environmental problems have become global problems.

CHANGE: HOW IT HAPPENS

Let's look briefly at the means by which we have made progress and how we need to continue to operate to build on our gains.

The improvements in our environment during the last 25 years have come from three forces operating together: education, legislation, and new technologies.

First, concerned individuals and groups mounted powerful campaigns to educate the public. From the first Earth Day in 1970, we have been deluged with information about the ecology of the Earth, air pollution, recycling, population growth, acid rain, toxic waste, the death of the oceans, and dozens of other topics. From books, magazine articles, and school and university programs to bumper stickers, buttons, and T-shirts, the environment has been a hot topic.

This education campaign worked on several fronts. It encouraged individuals to change their personal habits: "Instead of driving, try public transport or bicycling." "Don't throw that can or bottle away, recycle it." "Buy organic produce." "Plant a tree." It also helped to spawn the socially responsible investment movement, which puts pressure on corporations to alter their anti-environmental practices. Finally, because the voting population was more aware of environmental problems, political action groups could effectively lobby governments for regulatory change.

These new environmental regulations from federal, state, and local governments have been the second force in effecting change. During the last 25 years, Congress has enacted sweeping legislation designed to reduce the pollution of water, air, and earth. It even created an entire new body, the Environmental Protection Agency, to enforce these new laws.

At local levels, governments began to set up recycling programs and regulate what went into the dumps and landfills. Many communities went further, creating more nonpolluting public transportion, bike paths, toxic waste pickups, and educational programs about the environment.

Many of the new federal and state regulations were directed at industry, and this, along with pressure from private groups and individuals, has created the third force for improvement in the environment: new and improved technologies.

Two factors are remarkable in the response of corporate America to the new regulations: the first is the strength of the initial opposition to making the required changes; large corporations, especially, seem to have a knee-jerk policy of resisting any and all new regulations, regardless of how dire the need. They spend large amounts of their shareholders' money to argue that the required new technology is unworkable, impossible to achieve in the given time frame, and sure to cut profits and throw people out of work.

The second notable factor is the speed and efficiency with which these companies actually effect the necessary changes, once the new rules are in place. Often the innovative techniques actually save them money. These gains, however, don't prevent them from vigorously opposing the *next* regulation designed to protect and enhance the environment.

For example, for decades, American cars guzzled gasoline at the rate of about 8 to 18 miles per gallon (mpg); in 1973, the overall average was a miserable 13.3 mpg. Nevertheless, the automobile companies protested bitterly when new regulations were proposed in the 1970s to raise the mileage requirements. All the arguments listed were used and quite a few more. By 1986, however, Detroit was producing cars that got 20 to 35 mpg, with an average (for new cars) of 27.6 mpg. These cars still had plenty of pep and plenty of room inside but used half as much gas and produced much less pollution.

One would think that this progress would be a win-win-win situation for the consumers, the environment, *and* the auto manufacturers, who got a chance to appear environmentally concerned. Instead the big three automakers have joined with the oil companies in lobbying against any further increase in the mileage requirements.

Technology as a Friend

In contrast to the foot-dragging of the large corporations, some enterprising entrepreneurs saw the new regulations, coupled with the public interest in preserving the environment, as a great opportunity. If the old ways were wasteful and polluting, they would form companies to create new, improved products and services. If a newly aware public wanted to buy environmentally friendly products, they would produce and market them.

The managers of these companies are acting in the best tradition of free enterprise in that they see opportunities where others see problems. But while they may see an opportunity to make some money, most of these businesspeople are also environmentalists. They see the new technologies as a way to make a difference in the world.

These environmental entrepreneurs have begun to put a new face on technology. In spite of its many benefits, technology has traditionally played the role of a villain to many in the environmental field. To them, the private sector has appeared to be bent only on achieving technological "progress," that is, improving efficiency, with no regard for the effects on the physical or social environment.

Paying attention to these effects, however, changes technology from a villain to a valuable servant. A panel of photovoltaic cells, which produces electricity from sunlight with no noise or pollution, is a marvel of environmentally friendly technology. An automobile that runs on a nonpolluting fuel at the rate of 150 mpg is another.

The Impact of Technology

Clean air, clean water, clean soil: you don't get much argument when you speak of the benefits of an unpolluted environment. The arguments begin when you discuss how to achieve these benefits. What do we need to change? Do we have to give up much of our technology? How "clean" do we need to be?

Technology itself has often been accused of being the villain, as if a return to a more pastoral form of life would remedy the situation. But there has always been technology—ever since the first protohuman picked up a stick—and it has always impacted the environment. One theory about the extinction of the woolly mammoths in North America involves hunters with primitive technology—spears—arriving from Asia. All over the world, throughout history, farmers with only the most rudimentary tools have cut down forests and jungles and overcultivated the land, often with devastating effects on the local ecology.

On the other hand, it was such things as spears and primitive tools that allowed us to grow as a species. The benefits of technology are as apparent as its drawbacks. But until recently, all of our cleverness has gone into concentrating on the benefits, that is, improving our tools and machines. The drawbacks—the harmful effects on the land, air, water, and other species (not to mention our own species)—were largely ignored until the latter part of this century when they became too obvious to overlook.

The key, then, is not in the elimination of technology, but in its modification to better serve human needs and harmonize with the natural world. We can create this sustainable technology by focusing our attention on these goals.

These products, and many others like them, take the human and natural environments into account.

SUSTAINABLE TECHNOLOGY

The ultimate goal is to create techologies that not only sustain themselves, but also sustain life by giving back to the planet as much as they take. These sustainable technologies need to be created by what architect Sim Van der Ryn calls "smart design." This kind of design considers the best use of energy, resources, and people in the context of larger ecological patterns.

At present, because they are so new, environmental technologies are still fragmented into many different categories. But what Van der Ryn and other proponents of ecological design are talking about is planning on a larger scale. Paul Hawken, in *The Ecology of Commerce,* speaks of a future world economy that works ten times more efficiently.

How could this be possible? Doesn't our present, much-vaunted market economy operate at peak efficiency? No, it doesn't, and one reason is that very little planning went into its creation. You could say that it "just growed."

For example, petroleum products fuel most of our transportion system. But gasoline, which contains a very high energy content, is burned in our vehicles at dismal efficiencies of 13 percent to 18 percent. Petroleum is pumped from expensively drilled wells, transported thousands of miles, and refined into gasoline. Then it's burned at only 15 percent efficiency—and the by-products pollute the air.

This example should begin to illustrate the possible savings from a planned transportation system. As we will see in future chapters, the use of new, smart technologies, coupled with intelligent planning, has a multiplier effect on efficiency: one and one can often equal three, or five, or even ten.

Recycling Old Thought Patterns

In fact, we really have no choice but to adopt sustainable technologies. We have tended to think of our industrial system of production as the source of our wealth, but this is only partly true. The earth itself is the real source of our wealth; if we misuse its resources, they will dry up and we will become poor. Put in the language of investment, poisoning the ecosystem means destroying our capital.

The most important change in thinking, then, is to begin to see that our economic systems must mirror and cooperate with natural systems. Instead of living off the earth, taking whatever resources we need, we will live with it, returning what we take, and so becoming part of the natural cycle.

This way of thinking includes a revision of our either-or concept of the economy versus the environment. In fact, in addition to preserving our capital, sustainable technology eliminates much of the waste and inefficiency of our modern economies. This is smart economics. There are many other instances where shifts in thinking are needed, for example, "waste" is no longer waste, but resources to be used. Saving energy is not "conservation," but developing a new source of power, just as real as coal, gas, or solar power.

To reach our goal in 2050, we need to emerge from our twentieth century ways of perceiving the world and start thinking in these twenty-first century modes. *Sustainable, renewable, abundant,* and *harmonious* are some of the words that define this new way of thinking.

We will touch on these concepts as we discuss the new technologies throughout this book.

ECOLOGICAL BALANCE IN THE MIND

This book has two purposes. The first is to apprise investors of the various sustainable technologies and the companies that are working with them. As an investor, you have an unprecedented opportunity to vote with your capital for smart design and the firms that employ it. Included in this opportunity is a chance to increase your capital as the environmental economy grows.

The second purpose is to provide a counterbalance to the grim scenarios painted in the media and by many in the environmental field. There is no doubt that the problems we face are pretty awful. We are essentially involved in a race: can we deal with these issues before they overwhelm us?

There is no lack of material written on how badly the environment is being degraded and on the forces in government and industry which resist positive change. And this is important stuff; only by realizing just how bad things really are will we have the incentive to make real changes.

But concentrating solely on the degradation and the resistance to change can lead to despair—and, indeed, despair is an occupational hazard of those concerned with the environment. Innovative solutions to these problems deserve equal time. They engender hope and a feeling that we still have a chance to win the race.

These solutions—those that are already in place and those that are still in development—can provide a balance to our environmental sorrows. Their successes demonstrate not only that we can solve our difficulties and survive, but that we can create the kind of world we all want to live in—the world of 2050.

HOW THIS BOOK IS ARRANGED

After this introductory chapter, we're going to look at the broader field of socially responsible investing (SRI). This movement, which includes environmental investing, holds that your investment philosophy should be based on the same beliefs as the rest of your life. For example, if you believe that cigarette smoking is harmful, you will not invest in cigarette companies. While different people may have various social criteria for their investments, the SRI philosophy asks that these criteria be considered just as important as a return from an investment.

In chapter 3, we will then take a look at environmental investing in the context of the SRI movement. Again, it is your philosophy that governs your choice of environmental investments. If you want to support the environment in every way possible, then you may want to place a good portion of your capital in the stocks of companies that are actively working on solving environmental problems.

In chapters 4 through 13, we will focus on specific areas where new environmental technology is at work. Each chapter deals with a specific subject such as pollution, waste disposal, or transportation, which we will discuss in some detail.

There are two reasons for this attention to detail: first, for anyone interested in how humans can live in harmony with the planet, these various solutions make for fascinating reading. Not only can one admire their cleverness, but the hope they engender is inspiring. "Hey, we really *can* solve our problems if we work on it!"

The second reason is that investors in any field need to know as much about that field as possible. Learning the ins and outs of recycling or solar heating places you in the top ten percent of investors, that is, those who actually know something about the industry in which they're placing their precious capital. Joining this elite group greatly increases your chances of investment success.

In addition, environmentally concerned investors need to be able to distinguish between technologies which are truly sustainable and nonpolluting and those that are not. As the number of companies in the field grows, so does the number of products and practices that are called "green." If you take the trouble to invest in a socially resonsible manner, you will absolutely want to know that your capital is supporting the real stuff. This requires a certain level of knowledge about these new technologies.

At the end of each chapter, we discuss where to look for the the most promising companies in the featured sector and profile a few companies. Often, there are plenty of firms to investigate, but occasionally we come across exciting technologies that are so new that private industry has not yet caught up with them. In these cases, this book serves as an early warning system to investors; knowing about these innovative technologies will place you far ahead when they do arrive at the marketplace. If you watch, they will come!

In chapter 14, we go over the best way to invest in environmental companies, from mutual funds to individual stocks. We will discuss how you can greatly reduce your risk while optimizing your return. Also in chapter 14, you will discover the best places to find these environmental companies. In such a rapidly expanding sector, it's important to focus on the companies that are the most likely to succeed. The sources described in this chapter will help you do this.

Chapter 15 summarizes the ideas we have covered and takes a look at the future of sustainable practices.

Resources

The Ecology of Commerce: A Declaration of Sustainability. Paul Hawken. HarperCollins, 1993. $23.00 (also available in paperback).

For anyone who wants to know why things are the way they are in our national and world economies, this is the book. You will learn why, for example, in this corporate-dominated economy, it is often so difficult to make progress with programs that are earth-friendly and people-friendly.

This is in part because from the narrow viewpoint of profit-oriented corporations, such programs are irrelevant or hostile. But this focus on private gain leads to destructive environmental practices; the resulting damage to the world's ecosystems is vividly described. Hawken also includes plenty of valuable suggestions about how to deal with this apparent dichotomy between public good and private gain.

In short, this book will tell you what is happening, why it is happening, and what we can do about it.

The Green Disk. P.O. Box 32224, Washington, D.C. 20007.

This "paperless environmental journal" is filled with the best current thinking on the environment. Write to the address above to learn how to use your computer to access this information without being on-line.

International Ecological Design Society (IEDS) and The Natural Step U.S.

To create our vision of the next century, we're going to need all the brainpower we can muster. There are two organizations, one brand-new, the other new to this country, which are focusing a high level of intellect on designing systems that can exist in harmony with the planet.

International Ecological Design Society (IEDS). P.O. Box 11645, Berkeley, CA 94712. 510-869-5015. FAX: 415-332-5808. e-mail: ecodesign@igc.apc.org.

IEDS grew out of a conference held at Esalen (Big Sur, California) in October 1994. Attending were many well-known names in the environmental field, including Sim Van der Ryn, Paul Hawken, David Brower, and John Todd and Nancy Todd.

In the words of Interim Coordinator, Jacques Abelman, "The Society is dedicated to promoting ecological design, connecting those working in the grassroots with those in academia, government, the business world, and the design professions. It will foster research on issues of critical importance, forge convivial links, and create new educational opportunities."

IEDS plans to keep a World Wide Web site full of information and resources and to open an Internet conference group on ecological design. This is your best bet for keeping in touch with the cutting edge of environmental thought.

The Natural Step U.S. 17 Msgr. O'Brien Highway, Cambridge, MA 02141. 617-227-1199. FAX: 617-227-1648. e-mail: natstep@2nature.org.

The Natural Step was founded in Sweden in 1989 by oncologist Dr. Karl-Henrik Robert. If anyone can, this is the organization that can bridge the gap between private gain and public good. In Sweden, Robert started by getting consensus from top scientists on certain principles of environmental systems. A dialogue was then started with corporations, the government, and others with the intent of broadening this consensus. The results have been very encouraging; many businesses have subscribed to the sustainable principles of The Natural Step.

The Natural Step is now starting all over again in this country by building up a new consensus among scientists, businesspeople, and representatives from citizen and professional groups.

The Four System Conditions of The Natural Step:

1. Nature cannot withstand a systematic buildup of dispersed matter mined from the Earth's crust (oil, minerals, etc.).

2. Nature cannot withstand a systematic buildup of persistent compounds made by humans (such as organochlorines).

3. Nature cannot withstand a systematic deterioration of its capacity for renewal (such as the continued destruction of rain forests).

4. Therefore, if we want life to continue, we must (a) be efficient in our use of resources and (b) promote justice—because ignoring poverty will cause the poor to destroy resources we need (such as the rain forests), just so that they can survive.

CHAPTER 2

SOCIALLY RESPONSIBLE INVESTING

"Your article states that 'many analysts say this is a good time to buy cigarette-company stocks.' But if the cigarette companies continue hooking the people of the Third World, millions will sicken and die over the coming decades. Many are dying right now. Investing? This is more like profiting from a holocaust."

—SAMUEL CASE
NEWSWEEK, APRIL 18, 1994, "LETTERS"

The letter above was written in response to a *Newsweek* article about cigarette companies. Faced with a declining market in the U.S., and a clientele that has an unfortunate habit of dying prematurely, the large cigarette companies are spending much of their promotion efforts in developing countries. People in these countries are less aware of the diseases caused by cigarette smoke, and their governments are seduced by the prospects of tax revenues from the sale of tobacco products.

Meanwhile, a study published in *Lancet* in May 1995 has pushed the number of probable fatalities from smoking up to new highs; the Oxford-based study forecasts that *one-fifth* of the people now living in the developed countries may die prematurely of smoking-related diseases. This comes to about 250 million people. If you extrapolate these figures to the billions of people in developing countries where the cigarette companies are pushing their products, you attain a considerably higher figure.

On the other hand, that would mean a lot of cigarettes sold and large profits for the tobacco companies. Many companies are making good profits now; investors in Philip Morris have done very well over the past decade.

PHILOSOPHY AND INVESTING

Socially responsible investing (SRI)—also known as socially conscious investing or ethical investing—essentially asks investors to look at the gains from their investments and ask themselves if they want to profit from these activities. Do you want your investment to go up in value if it means that the company's profits come from products that make people sick—or cause ecological damage?

By choosing to be a socially responsible investor, you avoid investing in companies whose activities run counter to your values and beliefs. In this instance, SRI is an intensely personal matter; different investors will have different criteria. For some, companies that perform tests of products on animals are automatically excluded; others may choose to avoid firms that produce weapons.

There are no hard-and-fast rules in SRI; it's up to each individual to make the rules for his or her investments. Although SRI professionals have listed a number of criteria that can serve as guidelines for concerned investors, the final decision is always up to you.

Environmental investing is part of the SRI movement. As someone interested in sustainable technology companies, it can be very useful to you to understand the larger arena of social investing. SRI is one of the great socioeconomic movements of the times, one which has already made itself strongly felt in corporate boardrooms. In this chapter, we will look at SRI's successes and the directions it is heading in. But first, let's look at the different categories of SRI.

THREE CATEGORIES

There are three categories in socially responsible investing. The first involves the concept of "do no harm." Corporations in this category simply do not engage in activities that are harmful to people or the environment. They may not do anything to promote positive social change or environmental action, but investors can feel certain that their capital is not being used in any endeavors they would consider harmful.

Finding these companies involves screening out those firms whose products, services, or policies are considered harmful. For example, using guidelines commonly accepted by the SRI community, this "negative screen" would exclude investment in companies engaged in weapons sales or research, tobacco or alcohol, nuclear energy, or in testing products on animals. Major pollutors would be on the list as well as users of harmful chemicals (such as the ozone-depleting CFCs). In addition, firms with insensitive employment policies would be screened out.

Until 1994, firms that did business in South Africa were excluded by SRI screening. Now that apartheid has been abolished and Nelson Mandela is the head of a majority-ruled democracy in that country, that exclusion has been lifted. Many SRI professionals presently feel that investors should avoid companies doing business with Burma because of the repressive policies of the military junta in that country.

This negative screening still leaves a very large number of businesses to invest in. This is by far the largest category of SRI firms. When you see lists of socially responsible companies or check out the portfolios of SRI mutual funds, the majority are simply in this category of "do no harm."

The second category in SRI includes companies that actively promote positive change in society and/or the environment. Their products and services may fall simply in the "do no harm" category, but they may have innovative labor practices, lend support to charities, or be engaged in active environmental programs. In short, they are doing things that you, as a socially-concerned investor, might want to support.

Finding these firms involves using a "positive screen," that is, a screen that allows only firms with positive social or environmental policies to pass through. While there are fewer companies here than in the negative screen category, there are still plenty to invest in.

An example of a company in this positive category is AES Corporation, an independent power producer in Virginia. We're going to give a profile of AES later in this chapter as an examplary socially responsible company.

The third category in SRI is the one we are concerned with in this book. These are the firms whose products or services are designed to solve some pressing environmental problem. While the first two categories include corporations of all different sizes, these environmental companies are generally pretty small. This is because the field is still new; these firms have been formed to deal with problems that only recently have been recognized as problems.

Investing in environmental companies is *proactive* socially responsible investing. Whether you invest in a recycling company, an alternate energy firm, or others in the field, your capital is helping these firms develop and market their environmental technologies or services.

Investors need to be well aware that many products and practices that corporations may term "green" or "environmental" can actually be damaging to the environment. A waste management company may be disposing of toxic waste, but they might be doing it in an irresponsible manner, such as incineration. In this book, we plan to demonstrate just which methods called "environmental" are truly sustainable and which are not.

In order to build a successful portfolio, socially concerned investors need to consider companies in all three categories. As we will see in chapter 14, a successful SRI portfolio should include stocks of large and small firms in different fields. This spreads your risk and gives you the balance you need to weather financial ups and downs.

ETHICAL COMPLEXITIES

Using a negative screen to find companies that do no harm is relatively easy. The difficulties begin when you start trying to find companies in the second category using a positive screen. You are bound to find firms with, for example, innovative employee relations, but bad environmental records—or vice versa. There are several large utilities that are enthusiastic promoters of solar energy; unfortunately, they also have nuclear power plants on-line. And what about companies who sell to defense contractors, but these sales make up only a small percentage of their business?

Don't despair—socially concerned investors have a lot of help these days. At the end of this chapter, you will find some excellent books and newsletters to help guide you through the complexities of ethical investing. Several of these publications offer long lists of companies in different categories as well as SRI mutual funds. The newsletters, in particular, will direct you toward the most promising places to put your money.

Social Activism

We've talked about the personal side of responsible investing, that is, the importance of choosing investments that reflect your philosophy and values. But in choosing to invest your capital in certain companies— and withholding from others—you are also making a social statement. When your decisions are combined with those of millions of others of like mind, a powerful social movement is created.

SRI has its roots in the early part of this century when religious groups screened their investments for sin. Any company involved in gambling, liquor, tobacco, or pornography was blacklisted by these investors.

The modern SRI movement started in the late 1960s, in opposition to the Vietnam War. Student groups demanded that their universities sell all investments in companies producing war materials. Several mutual funds started in the early seventies excluded such companies and concentrated instead on firms friendly to the environment and to social change.

As a social movement, SRI sends a strong, negative message to firms engaged in harmful practices as well as encouragement to companies with positive social values. Boycotting a company's stock is roughly similar to boycotting its products.

SRI's effects have been steadily growing during the last 25 years. Initially dismissed by the investment establishment (*Fortune* magazine called it "insignificant do-good nonsense"), SRI has finally achieved respect.

This newfound respect has come partly as Wall Street professionals became aware of the growing amount of money invested with ethical considerations. This amount is presently estimated at $639 billion, or about 9% of the total invested in stocks, bonds, and mutual funds. The concerns of millions of SR investors has helped to create a climate in which corporate responsibility is now a valued commodity. In 1995, *Fortune*'s annual survey of "America's Most Admired Corporations" started with this statement: "There is a growing appreciation that corporations cannot live by numbers alone. Reputation is increasingly seen as something more than the record of earnings growth rates."

This report was significant in that of the eight criteria used in the study, only three were strictly financial. The others were quality of management, quality of products or services, ability to attract and keep talented people, *and responsibility to the community and the environment.*

Socially conscious investing has sent powerful messages not just to individual corporations, but to entire countries. Nelson Mandela has credited the continuous pressure to disinvest in South Africa as one of the most important factors in influencing the white-led government to back down. This was one of the great successes of SRI.

KEEPING UP THE PRESSURE

In 1989, a new level of investor activism was encouraged by the publication of the Valdez Principles. These are now called the CERES Principles, an acronym of the

Coalition for Environmentally Responsible Economies (see *Resources* for address).

CERES is a coalition of social investors, environmental groups, public pensions, and labor organizations. A company that endorses the CERES Principles pledges to monitor and improve its behavior in the following areas: protecting the biosphere, sustainable use of natural resources, reduction and disposal of wastes, energy conservation, risk reduction, safe products and services, environmental restoration, informing the public, and management commitments. Companies must also report on their progress with these pledges; this information is included in the annual CERES Report, which is available to the public.

CERES has made important advances. For one, the General Motors Corporation, along with others of the Fortune 500, has endorsed the CERES Principles. The Coalition is an excellent source for concerned investors. Shareholders, too, will have a powerful ally, when they encourage their companies to promote sustainable practices.

Keeping the pressure on corporate management is necessary partly because of the nature of corporations. These organizations are essentially designed to produce as much profit as possible for their shareholders. Managers who have a few lean years are often thrown out on their ears by irate stockholders.

This emphasis on short-term profits can run counter to funding the kind of long-term research necessary to develop sustainable technologies. The emphasis on the short-term bottom line requires that the technologies and methods already in place be milked for all they can produce.

Environmental pressure can take several forms. First it can come from government. We need to encourage our legislators to continue and increase well-planned environmental regulations directed at industry. Second, it can come from shareholders, who insist that the company adhere to guidelines such as the CERES Principles. Finally, individuals and environmental groups constantly need to remind managers that the public is very interested in corporate responsibility.

This latter kind of pressure can come from letter-writing campaigns, the exposure of harmful corporate practices, consumer boycotts, and disinvestment in the company's stock. It can also come from educating management. Many environmental leaders have met with corporate executives in an attempt to inform them of the benefits of sustainable practices. This is the kind of work that The Natural Step (see *Resources*, chapter 1) specializes in.

An enlightened board of directors can do a lot to convince shareholders that it is in the best interest of the company to pursue environmental policies. For proof that this is true, one only has to look at the growing number of companies, small and large, that are friendly to these kinds of policies. If the shareholders did not approve, they would vote the managers out of office.

As a prime example of activism at the top, we're going to look at AES, a large electric power producer that has incorporated environmental action and concern for the community into the way it does business. This company is living proof that excellent profits can go hand in hand with ecological awareness. Because of this, AES has become a model that other companies can emulate to their advantage.

AES CORPORATION

Imagine a company whose management felt that every decision had to be made not just with profit in mind, but also environmental considerations, employee satisfaction, fairness to suppliers, and the welfare of the surrounding community. Imagine no further; this describes the Applied Energy Services (AES) Corporation, an independent power producer centered in Arlington, Virginia.

AES is one of the world's largest independent power producers; its revenues totaled $533 million in 1994. It runs power plants in six states and four plants in three foreign countries; six more facilities are near completion, three in the U.S. and three in India and Pakistan. In addition, the company has a 40 percent share in the AES China Generating Company, which will develop power projects in China.

In spite of the size of the corporation, the cofounders of AES believe that its 550 employees should play a large part in managing the firm. "There isn't a single piece of data that I have that isn't accessible to every other person in the company," says CEO Dennis Bakke. Employees rotate responsibilities and teams of workers take on such jobs as negotiating financing for new power projects. Bakke and Chairman Roger Sant have the novel belief that employees should enjoy themselves on the job. Consequently, morale is high and turnover is almost nonexistent.

On the environmental front, although AES power plants burn fossil fuels, their emissions of such pollutants as nitogen oxide and sulphur dioxide run an average of 58 percent below permitted levels. This kind of commitment to the environment is considered an integral part of AES by the management and employees.

For example, when Roger Sant became concerned over the contribution to global warming of the carbon dioxide emitted from company power plants, AES decided to fund a program of tree planting. The goal is to plant enough trees to absorb all the carbon dioxide produced by AES's new coal-burning plants over their

30- to 40-year lifetimes. A project for planting 52 million trees is presently underway in Guatemala.

In Paraguay, a joint venture with the Nature Conservancy will preserve 143,000 acres of threatened forest land. And in Ecuador, Bolivia, and Peru, a ten-year project with Oxfam America will help indigenous Amazonian Indians gain title to—and assist them in the management of—3.7 million acres of their traditional lands.

Such ambitious projects do not seem to have hurt AES's bottom line. The company has shown consistent growth in revenues and earnings for the last eleven years. Net profits were up 28 percent in 1993 and 33 percent in 1994. As you might imagine from these figures, the company is very popular with most Wall Street analysts.

Companies such as AES support erroneous arguments such as the notion that environmental and social concerns run counter to profits. This corporation has become a model to which socially aware investors can compare the performance of other corporations.

Resources

Business Ethics. Bi-monthly. $49.00/year. Subscription Dept., P.O. Box 14748, Dayton, OH 45413-9932. 800-601-9010.

This is a great magazine for both business managers and social investors. American businesses—large and small—are presently in the midst of radical change as they struggle to compete while also becoming more responsive to consumers, employees and the environment. You will learn about the latest trends in progressive business, and the companies which are making them work. There is an excellent section for social investors, including profiles of promising, publicly traded companies. Highly recommended.

CERES (The Coalition for Environmentally Responsible Economies). 711 Atlantic Avenue, Boston, MA 02111.

To learn more about CERES and The CERES Principles, send $5.00 for their information packet. You can support the Principles by becoming a contributing member. CERES also publishes a quarterly newsletter, *On Principle* ($25.00/year). You will get a sample copy with the information packet.

The Clean Yield. 41 Old Pasture Road, Greensboro Bend, VT 05842-2102. 802-533-7178. Six issues: $80.00/year. Trial issue: $3.00.

The Clean Yield is an asset management company specializing in SRI. If, however, you don't have the required minimum of $250,000 in assets, I would highly recommend *The Clean Yield* newsletter.

Companies profiled in *The Clean Yield* are researched for weapons production, environmental practices, labor and community relations, affirmative action, tobacco production, gambling, nuclear power generation, animal testing, human rights, and executive compensation as well as financial performance. Each company profile portrays the company's financial prospects and then describes how the company handles social factors (such as those previously listed).

In addition, there are updates on companies previously profiled and a list of about thirty SR companies, divided into investment categories of conservative, moderate, and aggressive. Also included are articles about SRI and the state of the stock market.

Hulbert's Financial Digest, which rates the performance of investment newsletters, reported that *The Clean Yield* was one of just fourteen newsletters that outperformed the market in 1992 and for the five-year period ending in December, 1992. Investors should find this fine publication very useful.

Co-op America. 1612 K Street NW, #600, Washington, D.C. 20006. 202-872-5307. Individual membership: $20.00/year; business membership starts at $60.00/year.

Anyone interested in SRI and sustainable development needs to belong to Co-op America. Through a number of programs and publications, this organization aims to: "educate people about how to use their spending and investing power to bring the values of social justice and environmental responsibility into the economy." They are also dedicated to helping SRI companies and putting pressure on irresponsible firms.

Membership brings a free copy of the *National Green Pages*, a directory of thousands of environmental and socially responsible businesses, both small and large. You will also receive their quarterly magazine, which includes useful articles about SRI, environmental firms, boycotts of certain products, and consumer information. This is an excellent resource at a bargain price.

Franklin Research's Insight. Monthly. $195/year. Franklin Research and Development, 711 Atlantic Avenue, Boston, MA 02111. 617-423-6655. e-mail: FRDC@igc.apc.org. Ask for sample copies.

Franklin Research's Insight gives specific recommendations on SR companies. This service includes a newsletter on SRI, *Investing for a Better World,* which is available by itself for $29.95/year.

There are reports on SR mutual funds, but I see the *Insight* as being primarily valuable for those who want to invest in SR individual stocks. The reports on several companies featured each month are professional and thorough. A fine service for serious investors.

GOOD MONEY Quarterly Reports. Quarterly. $36.00/year. Good Money Publications, Box 363, Worcester, VT 05682. 800-535-3551 (same for FAX). e-mail customer service and inquiries: ambx79a@prodigy.com.

GOOD MONEY was founded by one of the pioneers of SRI, Ritchie Lowry. Lowry has also written *GOOD MONEY: A Guide to Profitable Social Investing in the '90s* (W. W. Norton, 1991, 1993), an excellent overview of SRI.

GOOD MONEY is more like an information newsletter about SRI than it is an investment newsletter. In addition to profiles of companies, there are articles of general interest to the socially conscious investor. They do not give "buy, sell, and hold" recommendations. Rather, in their own words, they "provide sufficient information so that informed investors and consumers can make their own judgements. . . ."

Good Money Publications also puts out a biannual *Guide to the Socially Screened Funds,* with interim year updates. And

Good Money hosts a forum on the World Wide Web (see *Resources*, chapter 3) Investors interested in SRI would do well to get involved with this organization of experts.

The Greenmoney Journal. Quarterly. $35.00/year, $50.00/two years. Attn. Subscriptions, West 608 Glass Ave., Spokane, WA 99205. 509-328-1741.

The Greenmoney Journal, like *GOOD MONEY,* presents excellent articles about SRI, together with some information about specific companies. The journal includes useful features such as a Performance Update for SR mutual funds, a Green Events calendar, and a list of publications of interest to the SR investor.

In September, 1995, *Greenmoney* started a home page on the World Wide Web for socially responsible investors. Categories at this site include Natural Products, Technology, Investing, Sustainable Building and Energy Resources, Eco Travel, and others. There are also valuable links to other pertinent web sites. http://www.greenmoney.com.

The *Greenmoney Journal* is an excellent resource for the concerned investor—well-written and full of useful information.

Investing from the Heart: The Guide to Socially Responsible Investments and Money Management. Jack A. Brill and Alan Reder. Crown Publishers, 1992, revised 1993. $12.00, paperback.

This is one of my favorite books on SRI. It covers the basics of all kinds of socially responsible investments in a clear, readable style. Jack Brill is a financial consultant with First Affirmative Financial Network and Alan Reder is a freelance writer. (Reder now has a new book on ethical business practices: *In Pursuit of Principle and Profit.*)

This book is equally useful to small and large investors. Highly recommended.

CHAPTER 3

ENVIRONMENTAL INVESTING

Many people invest in a disconnected manner, attempting to choose the best investments solely on their financial merits. These same people would probably not choose a profession just for the money: they would choose a field they were interested in and believed in—something in which they could really involve themselves.

Ideally, investing should come from a similar place; what you invest in should be an expression of who you are. This is more than just a pretty concept: it will most likely turn you into a better investor. The more interesting an investment is to you, the more likely you are to do the necessary research before you put any money into a company; you're also more likely to stay in touch once you own the stock. It is this involvement that makes successful investors.

Peter Lynch, the manager of the immensely successful Fidelity Magellan Fund during the 1980s, talks about "immersing himself " in all the information about any company he is thinking of buying. Those who are interested in preserving the environment should find it easy to immerse themselves in information about environmental companies.

We're going to talk about the world of 2050 in greater detail in this chapter. This is so that you, as an investor in environmental companies, can see clearly just how your capital can help create this new world. Sustainable technology is going to be instrumental in the making of a positive future; the more capital environmental firms can gather, the faster and better they can do the necessary research.

Sustainable technology will even have a large role in solving such seemingly intractable problems as poverty and overpopulation. We will cover these subjects at the end of the chapter.

2050 C.E. AGAIN

Let's return for now to our vision of the next century—a future in which clean air, water, and soil are taken for granted and in which there is an abundance of energy and raw materials. What would be required to reach this environmental utopia?

In 2050, most of our power needs will come from nonpolluting sources. No nuclear power, no acid rain–producing coal, and very little oil. (We will probably still need some oil for certain industrial processes, unless radical new technology emerges.) But low oil consumption will mean an end to most pollution from hydrocarbons, no budget-busting oil imports, and no wars over decreasing supplies.

Instead, electric power for homes, industry, and transportation will come from a combination of photovoltaics (electricity from the sun), wind energy, and hydropower. This is not an unrealistic scenario. All the technology is already here and working; we're simply talking about scaling it up.

Virtually all waste products will be either reused or recycled. Sewage is processed into organic fertilizer and food garbage into either fertilizer or animal feed. In the case of hard goods, the company that fabricates a product takes responsibility for it from "cradle to grave." Whatever small quantities of materials cannot be recycled are disposed of safely.

All food will be produced without the use of chemicals. Most fertilizers will come from the organic composting of garbage, and pest control is achieved using natural methods. Without contaminating chemicals from agriculture, industry, municipal dumps, and septic systems, the soil is clean and the oceans, rivers, and lakes are sparkling and full of life.

Through the use of sensible irrigation practices on farms and inexpensive water-saving devices in homes, there is no more need for expensive, environmentally damaging water projects.

In the year 2050, forests are regrowing all over the world. This is largely because trees are no longer used to make paper. A variety of tough, fast-growing plants has taken their place, with great savings, both financially and environmentally. And even the acreage required for cultivating these plants is relatively small because most paper is recycled. Although there is still a need for wood products, these come from selective cutting in the forests or well-managed tree plantations.

Metals are mined in an environmentally friendly manner, and after the mines are closed, the landscape is returned to as close to the original state as possible. Industrial production is also safe and nonpolluting.

The exciting thing about this vision of the twenty-first century is that much of the technology necessary to make this world a reality is already being employed.

What is required is simply to continue perfecting the innovative technologies and to expand their use—to phase out the old ways and bring in the new.

In each of chapters 4 through 13, we're going to cover a new industry that is working on one of the technologies listed previously. From photovoltaics to garbage, from organic food to copper mining, we're going to show how each new technology brings our vision of 2050 closer to realization.

We're also going to look at specific companies that are working in these environmental fields now. And last, but not least, we will discuss the possibilities for investment in each field.

STAYING CURRENT

Speaking of investments, the companies profiled here have been chosen because they represent prime examples of the new technologies. As of this writing, they also look like good investments, but by the time you read this, the situation may have changed. While the environmental field, as a whole, should remain very attractive to investors, you should check the most recent news about any companies you may see here before you consider buying into them. You may read this book a year or more after publication, by which time the market and the companies may have gone through significant changes.

By the time you read this, for example, investors may have decided that some of the firms described here are the hottest things going and driven their stock up to unrealistic levels. A few companies may be having problems, making them unattractive to investors, while others may still be very attractive. Investors should choose specific companies by relying on only the most up-to-date information from newsletters, advisers, company repre-

"Environmental" Companies

In order to attract the increasing numbers of socially conscious investors (and customers), some companies are falsely passing themselves off as environmental. Many large corporations tend to advertise their concerns for the environment while continuing to pollute and to lobby against government regulations.

Some non-SRI mutual funds also call themselves "environmental," although their holdings may include companies with terrible records of pollution. Investors should check out the list of true SRI mutual funds in the appendix and remain aware that snake oil remains a major pollutant in the marketplace.

sentatives, and other good, current sources. In chapter 14, we'll discuss in detail how to find the best environmental firms.

POPULATION, POVERTY, AND SUSTAINABLE TECHNOLOGY

No book on the environment would be complete without some mention of poverty and the growth of global population. Many people fear that uncontrolled growth, particularly in developing countries, will place such demands on the ecosystem that it will be irreparably damaged, bringing about mass starvation and disease.

But population experts have noticed that as people grow more secure and prosperous, birthrates tend to fall. Birthrates in the industrialized nations are generally at

Population: How Serious a Problem?

A graph of world population growth shows a long, steady growth curve ranging from about 1 billion people in the year 1800 to about 2.5 billion in 1950. Then, in 1950, the curve suddenly begins to spike upward, reaching over 5 billion by 1990 and continuing on up the chart to a projected 8.5 billion in 2020. Ninety percent of this growth is taking place in developing countries.

As a case in point, Nigeria had a population of 43 million in 1950; by 1990 this had doubled to 86 million. By the year 2000, Nigeria is projected to have 160 million people, and by 2020, 273 million.

By 2020, India is expected to have 1.2 billion people, which is four to five times the current population of the U.S. on one-third the land.

Given the limited amount of land and resources in the developing world, most people agree that continued population growth will be a major problem in the world.

replacement levels; population is even falling in some countries.

Two reasons for the current levels of population growth in less prosperous countries are lack of education and inavailability of birth control. Other reasons are that children are seen as another set of working hands for a family—and as insurance for the parents in old age. As families grow financially more secure, the need for more children lessens.

One of the greatest problems in developing nations is that their resources—land, labor, and materials—are often used more for the benefit of a wealthy elite than for the majority of the population. For example, traditional farming practices, which encouraged diversified food crops, have been replaced with one-crop, export-oriented plantation farming. While this may enrich the few who own the land, along with the multinational food corporations, this system tends to keep the workers in poverty. It also is bad ecology—one-crop agriculture tends to degrade the land and requires massive doses of chemical fertilizer and pesticides.

Problems like these, of course, are as much social and political as environmental. But this kind of plantation socioeconomic system keeps masses of people in poverty, and poverty leads to the kind of population growth that limits resources, degrades the environment, and ultimately causes more poverty.

The kinds of environmental technology discussed in this book can be used by people in the developing world as part of their struggle to break out of the cycle of poverty. Real sustainable development can grow from this right use of technology.

Several of the firms profiled in later chapters are working in developing countries. Some are planting trees; others are installing renewable energy devices in villages. Planting trees, for example, is a simple way to improve the soil and provide a source of wood for varied uses.

The use of solar, wind, and water power helps local economies in two ways. First, providing inexpensive sources of power for such crucial activities as cooking and pumping water, frees labor for other productive tasks. Second, instead of being spent for expensive oil or other fuel, money is retained in the local economy.

The recycling methods detailed in chapters 6 and 7 can be used to good effect in developing countries. Recycling is a labor-intensive activity that can create jobs in local economies as well as provide a cheap source of raw materials. And the many specialty crops, which can be grown profitably on a small scale (described in chapter 8), can bring income to village farmers.

There are numerous, far-seeing nonprofit organizations that are trying to encourage sustainable practices in the developing world. But there is also a place for the private sector in this endeavor, for the kind of companies profiled in this book. Readers who are concerned about poverty and population growth in the Third World will want to pay special attention to these firms—and watch for other, similar companies.

Resources

For newsletters dealing with specific investments in the environmental field, see *Resources* in chapter 14.

In Business. Bimonthly. $29.00/year, $49.00/two years. 419 State Avenue, Emmaus, PA 18049. 610-967-4135.

In Business covers environmentally oriented businesses and technologies. It's a must for environmental investors because it will allow you to keep up-to-date on what's happening in environmental technologies.

Many of the businesses discussed in the magazine are too small to be publicly traded, but there are always a few interesting public companies in each issue. Jack Brill (*Investing from the Heart*) and his son, Hal, have a column for investors that profiles a promising company with stock you can buy.

The Green Connection™

The folks at *GOOD MONEY,* the newsletter mentioned in *Resources*, chapter 2, now host a forum for environmental businesses on the PRODIGY network. There are more than a dozen topics including Energy, Recycling, and Organic Farming. To join the discussion, from PRODIGY, [jump] "green connect" and click on "Bulletin Board."

CHAPTER 4

THE COSMIC POWER AND LIGHT COMPANY

L et's fine-tune a lens for our vision of the year 2050. Zeroing in on the buildings of that time, we see that the roofs are all fabricated from some dark, glossy material. What we are seeing is a material that was first coming into use at the end of the twentieth century. At that time, when most solar panels were free-standing or were bolted to roofs, several researchers got the bright idea of building photovoltaic material directly into roofing materials.

So what we are seeing in 2050 are roofs that not only keep out the weather and keep in the heat, but also produce electricity. Photovoltaic material is even built into window glass! In addition, piping built into other areas of the roof produces hot water for space heating and domestic use.

Seen from the perspective of the next century, our present system of centralized power plants distributing electricity by means of thousands of miles of wires looks very primitive. We burn expensive, polluting fuel to power generators, transmit the power to buildings, then convert the electricity back to light, heat, and mechanical power.

This system is very inefficient compared to free power from the sun, delivered at no cost directly to our homes. Our roof-based power system of the future converts the light into electricity and heat, cleanly and quietly, and stores it for use at night and on sunless days.

Now, get ready for a crash course in solar technology in the next few pages. This is the kind of information you will need before you try buying stock in any solar-oriented company. Remember that successful investors are savvy investors.

Right now there are only a few small public companies in the solar field, but in a few years there are going to be dozens. So some of what you learn here will simply prepare you for the new technologies when they arrive at the marketplace.

PHOTOVOLTAICS

In the early 1950s, scientists at Bell Laboratories fabricated the first photovoltaic (PV) cell. When exposed to sunlight, these small, flat silicon-based devices converted the light into electricity. The voltage was very small, but when connected to other cells, useful amounts of electricity were produced. Bell Telephone soon put the new technology to work powering remote relay stations. And later the growing space program placed arrays of photovoltaic cells on its satellites.

Alternative energy enthusiasts (like this author) were soon envisioning scenarios like the one described in this chapter, that is, photovoltaics as a primary source of clean power. But development was maddeningly slow. Electricity from the sun was not yet cost-effective; the cells didn't produce enough voltage per unit cost to compete with utility-based power. Through the 1960s and 1970s, we watched as production costs slowly fell and conversion efficiencies slowly rose (conversion efficiency measures the amount of sunlight actually changed into electric current).

From the 1980s up to the present, the cost of photovoltaics has fallen precipitously. This is due partly to new technology, partly to the economics of scale as more PV cells are produced. This progress creates a positive trend: as the price falls, more applications for the cells become practical, then, as more cells are produced, the manufacturing costs per cell fall still further.

State-of-the-art PV batteries now retail for about $5 to $7 per watt. This price makes photovoltaics competitive with utility power for many homes in remote locations. Installing a photovoltaic system, complete with storage batteries, often costs less than running utility lines into the property. There are now about 100,000 PV-powered homes in the U.S. and an equal number in developing countries.

In addition, the cells are appearing in many new places. Emergency phones on many highways are powered by PV panels. The military has a mobile power system for communications in the field. In a growing number of villages in developing countries, small PV arrays are powering water pumps and lighting systems. This is a technology whose time has finally arrived.

UTILITIES

There will still be a need for utility-based power in the future. The roofs of multistory buildings simply do not have the area to fit enough solar cells to fulfill the power needs of the occupants. Even if photovoltaic materials were built into the exterior walls and windows, large buildings would still need additional power. Most manufacturing plants also need much more electrical power than they can generate from their rooftops.

Utilities will be able to fulfill these needs, however, using their own combination of nonpolluting, renewable energy sources. These will include large PV arrays, wind generators, hydropower, and geothermal power. Some utilities have already added wind generators to their systems, and a few are working with PV arrays. Others are beginning to buy power from small, independent renewable energy producers.

The utilities will be able to generate all the power they need from renewables because the demand on their generating capacity will be much less. This will be partly because of the millions of high-voltage rooftops, partly because of greatly increased energy efficiency. In chapter 11, we will cover the enormous savings that increased energy efficiency will bring.

For now, we will simply point out that large amounts of power will be saved as energy-efficient buildings, vehicles, electric motors, and lighting become commonplace. And the demand for power will be further reduced when recycling becomes the norm. Fabricating new products from recycled materials generally requires anywhere from a third to a half less energy than using raw materials.

As the price of solar cells falls and air quality requirements rise, utilities are beginning to look at large-scale PV power. The Sacramento Municipal Utility District in California is installing PV systems on rooftops at the rate of 100 per year. Since they started in 1993, the installed cost of the arrays has fallen from $7.00 to $5.00 per watt ($5.00 per watt = $.50 per kilowatt/hour).

It's important to remember that most environmental technology is still in its infancy. PV is a good illustration

Let's Get Our Electrical Measurements Straight

A watt (W) is a measure of electric power. If the bulb in your lamp is 100 watts, it takes 100 watts of power to light it. A thousand watts is one kilowatt (kW). One kilowatt/hour (kWh) is a measure of 1,000 watts operating for one hour. If you turn on ten 100 watt bulbs, after an hour you will have used 1 kilowatt/hour of electricity (10×100 W = 1,000 W = 1 kW).

The kilowatt/hour is used by your power company in determining your monthly payment. If you check your bill, you will find electrical use measured in kWh. An average American home, without electric heat, might use anywhere from 10 to 20 kWh per day, or 300 to 600 kWh per month.

One megawatt = 1,000 kilowatts, or 1,000,000 watts. Megawatts (MW) are more convenient to use when speaking of utility-size power production. For example, to power 1,000 homes, each using an average of 15 kW per day, a utility would have to generate 15 MW per day (1,000 W $\times$ 15 = 15,000 kW = 15 MW).

The quantity of electricity used in the U.S. is about 2.5 trillion kWh per year.

of this. While much of the PV industry is still operating at costs of around 50 cents per kWh for small projects, several recent breakthroughs may radically reduce this figure, at least for larger operations.

In 1994, Enron Corporation, a major natural gas company, bid to develop 100 megawatts of PV power in the Nevada desert. This area is part of a Solar Enterprise Zone run by the U.S. Department of Energy at a nuclear test site. What shocked the PV industry was the price at which Enron said they could deliver the power: 5.5 cents per kWh. Enron Corporation spokespersons speak guardedly of a new, proprietary technology that will make this price possible; economies of scale also enter into this picture.

EFFICIENCY AND COST-EFFECTIVENESS

The efficiency of PV cells ranges anywhere from 5 percent to 20 percent. This figure measures how much of the sunlight striking the cell actually gets converted into electric power. Solar engineers get excited when the possibility is mentioned of reaching efficiencies higher than 20 percent. But here we have a couple of new technologies that have the possibility of going far beyond 20 percent.

TU Electric, a major Texas utility, is experimenting with a PV collector that concentrates the sunlight on a thin strip of PV cells. Built by ENTECH, Inc., of Dallas, this collector uses a Fresnel lens to concentrate the sun 21 times. This means greatly reduced costs for the PV cells, usually the most expensive element. Other costs go up, however, for such elements as the lens and the tracking system necessary to keep the sunlight focused on the cells.

ENTECH's collectors are 3 feet wide and 12 feet long; 72 of them comprise a "solar row," which will produce 30 kW in bright sunlight. The company has several installations, including one at TU Electric's Energy Park, near Dallas, which will eventually produce 300 kW.

Using totally different technology, there is a possibility that a thin film called Lumeloid™ may put the game into another ballpark. This technology mimics the photosynthetic process of plants and may have the capability of reaching efficiencies of *80 percent*. Such is the speed of progress, now that some real money is going into research and development of renewable power.

At the same time, it's important to realize that efficiency, while important, is secondary to cost. A 10 percent efficient system may need to cover twice the area as a system with 20 percent efficiency, but if its manufacturing cost is less per watt produced, then this will likely be the system employed.

It's particularly important for investors not to get carried away by impressive-sounding technologies. For example, both the Lumeloid™ film and the ENTECH concentrating collectors may turn out to be so expensive to manufacture that they will price themselves out of the market. In the end, it will be the most cost-effective technologies that capture the markets.

SOLAR STEAM

Also in the running in the solar division is "solar steam." This kind of energy is created by concentrating the sun's rays to run a heat engine that turns an electric generator. Solar steam is another of those systems that generally requires utility-sized resources. There are a few small units available that focus sunlight by means of a parabolic dish mirror (similar in appearance to a satellite television dish), but most of the research and development has gone into large systems.

The solar concentrating collectors in these large arrays are shaped like long troughs and focus the sunlight on a pipe. The working fluid in the pipe is circulated to a generating station where it heats water into steam to run a turbine-powered generator. Air-powered heat engines called Stirling-cycle engines are also being perfected; they may replace the steam turbines for some applications.

The operating technology may be more complex than that of photovoltaics, but up to now, it has proven more cost-effective. During the 1980s, an Israeli company called Luz International constructed nine solar thermal plants in California's Mojave Desert. Luz has since reorganized under the name of Solel, but the solar collectors are still producing 350 MW of power. Southern California Edison buys the electricity at an average cost of 11.2 cents per kWh.

There are a number of other solar thermal concepts. The most promising of these involves a tall central tower surrounded by several acres of mirrors. The mirrors are all positioned to focus sunlight on a receiver on the tower; this receiver can get as hot as 1,300°F, high enough to efficiently run a steam generator. Experiments in many countries with central-receiver power plants have been encouraging; this could become one of the most cost-effective solar technologies.

As the cost of PV cells falls, the simplicity of this technology may win out over the solar steam plants. Solel, and others, however, are working on innovations that may lower the cost of solar thermal power to as little as 6 cents per kWh. Whichever technology "wins" in the long run—and it may be that both will prove cost-effective in different applications—the consumer and the environment will be the final winners.

POWER STORAGE

As you may have noticed, the one little problem with both photovoltaic and solar thermal power is that the sun doesn't shine all the time. This means that either there must be a backup source of energy or that power must be stored for nighttime and cloudy days. Houses run by PV power have batteries to store electricity, but this is not practical for large-scale operations.

Storage is not as serious a problem as it may appear. Less electricity is used at night and a utility usually gets power from other sources that can fill in. Hydropower and geothermal power, for example, run night and day; wind power, though less reliable, can often fill in. The solar thermal plants in the Mojave Desert are run by low-polluting natural gas when the sun is gone.

There have been many fancy schemes devised to store power. Pumping water up into a lake and using the falling water to power generators on demand is a method already used by a few utilities. An Alabama utility pumps air into a giant underground cavern; the compressed air then powers a turbine to generate electricity when needed. Storing the sun's heat by day in various substances and using the heat to power steam generators at night has been tried with some success.

It's difficult to store solar energy at temperatures high enough to run a steam generator efficiently. But how about storage for heating? This is easier because the temperatures required are not so high. Buildings in several communities in Sweden have solar collectors mounted on their rooftops. Pumps circulate a fluid heated by the summer sun through the collectors, then through enormous piles of buried crushed rock or underground pools. During the winter, this stored summer warmth is used to supply a district heating system.

All these storage methods are low-tech, however, compared to superconducting magnetic energy storage (SMES). A SMES system involves pumping electricity into a coil of wire as large as half a mile across. This wire has been cooled to $-270°C$; the low temperatures are what give it the superconducting storage capacity. In the U.S., the Departments of Energy and Defense have been experimenting with a 10 MW SMES system.

Hydrogen can be used not only as a fuel, but also as an excellent storage medium. Because hydrogen can be made by running an electric current through water, one section of a PV array could be put to work making hydrogen during the day. The hydrogen would then power an electric generator or fuel cells during the night. We will discuss this advanced, nonpolluting technology more thoroughly in chapter 9. Hydrogen has many characteristics which, at present, make it appear the best candidate for storing sunlight.

DISTRIBUTION

How would this "clean" power be distributed? One scenario involves keeping the present utility grid system in which power lines run to all buildings. PV arrays on each building would feed electric power into the system when the sun was out and take power from it on cloudy days or at night.

Another way would be to have only those buildings with large power needs connected to the grid. All others would have their own storage system of batteries or other more advanced storage systems presently in development. The PV cells would charge the storage system when the sun was out, and the house would be powered from storage at night. This is how present-day all-solar houses operate.

SOLAR HEATING

In the 1970s, the federal government enacted generous tax credits for companies involved in renewable energy. Individuals who installed solar heating systems also received tax benefits. These programs came in the wake of the oil shortages and price increases caused by the oil embargo of 1973 and the pricing policies of the OPEC cartel. Their purpose was to encourage the development of alternate energy sources and decrease our dependence on oil.

One of the unfortunate results of the tax credits, however, was to nurture poorly designed and cost-ineffective technology. The solar heating systems and wind generators built in the 1970s were not actually competitive in the energy marketplace. This became apparent once the tax credits were withdrawn in the 1980s; most of the small companies producing these systems went under. Wind generator farms languished, and many consumers were left with leaky, inefficient solar heating systems.

It's possible to argue that any new technology goes through first generation failures and that some form of government assistance is necessary in the early stages. But in this case, particularly with solar heating systems, the public was left with a bad impression, which the solar industry has been working hard to overcome.

This is especially unfortunate because the sun is a very cheap and effective way of heating water for domestic use. In Japan, there are 1.5 million solar water heaters in Tokyo alone; in Israel, two-thirds of all homes use this simple technology.

What happens when the sun goes in? Most systems have storage capacity but after this is used up, your regular water heater simply kicks in. The solar unit is almost always linked with a gas or electric unit. Even with these added fuel costs, however, the savings can be substantial; depending on the climate, a well-designed solar heater can provide anywhere from 50 percent to 90 percent of domestic hot water.

SPACE HEATING

In the 1970s, many people were excited about the prospect of heating buildings using solar heat. Quite a few

---

Victorian Solar Heaters

A little-known fact is that there was a solar boom in Southern California in the 1890s. By 1900, there were a million homes with solar water heaters as well as 300,000 swimming pools heated by the sun.

Utilities countered this threat by offering free natural gas hook-ups. Natural gas was very cheap at that time and this, added to the fact that most solar systems were not designed to cope with occasional freezing weather, eventually convinced most home-owners to switch to gas.

---

complex and expensive systems were devised, involving the circulation of a working fluid through solar collectors on rooftops. These "flat-plate" collectors consisted of loops of copper piping bonded to black sheet metal, with a glass cover. In direct sunlight, the fluid in the pipes would be heated to anywhere from 120°F to 180°F.

The heated fluid then circulated through a storage tank at ground-floor level, transferred its heat to the water in the tank, and returned to the collectors. The water in the storage tank was used to heat the house.

In spite of much enthusiasm and some fancy technology, most of these systems foundered on the rocks of cost and unreliability. Without the solar tax credits, most solar systems simply could not save enough in heating costs to justify their initial expense. Add numerous equipment breakdowns to this equation and consumers began to lose interest very quickly.

Also at that time information about energy conservation was beginning to come out. It became clear that adding insulation to a building was the most cost-effective way of reducing heating expenses (see chapter

11). The answer was not to bring in more heat, but to hold on to the heat that was already there.

Architects began to realize that instead of the roof-top collectors, pumps, and storage systems of the so-called active solar heating systems, they could design passive systems, which used the building itself as the collector and the storage unit. Collectors on passive solar houses are large windows that face south to take full advantage of the sun. The heat storage systems are integral parts of the house, such as dark slate floors, which are warmed by the sun and stay warm well into the night.

This is not a new concept; the ancient Greeks situated their homes to take advantage of the Mediterranean sun. And adobe dwellings in the southwest United States have thick walls, which absorb the sun's heat by day, then release it slowly to the interior during the cool desert nights. By morning, the walls are cool enough to provide a buffer against the daytime heat. This is passive solar storage at its best.

There are still a few active solar space-heating systems on the market, but the emphasis has shifted to total building design, which makes the energy systems an integral part of the building. Conservation of energy is emphasized, passive solar heat is maximized in cool climates, and the result is greatly lowered energy costs.

THE MANY USES OF SOLAR

In industrial applications where heat is required, solar can be substituted for fossil fuels in almost every instance. Low-grade heat is easy to generate, but very high temperatures can also be attained through the use of concentrating collectors. This means that solar-generated heat may be used for many industrial processes.

These high temperatures require high-tech equipment, but even the lowest-tech solar can attain temperatures high enough to cook food. Using the simplest of materials—wood, cardboard, aluminum foil, and glass—you can build a small solar oven that will cook food at temperatures from 300°F to 400°F. In the developing world, where villagers often spend days gathering firewood to cook with, these ovens can change people's lives.

But solar ovens are not just for the developing world. If you don't feel like building one, you can buy a ready-made model for $100 or more and start making solar casseroles and solar bread. Not only will you conserve gas or electricity, but solar oven chefs swear that the food tastes better!

One of the most popular forms of solar energy is swimming pool heating. Whether the low-cost collectors are used for small pools or large municipal pools, the heating bills are lowered dramatically. And, with the addition of a pool cover, the swimming season can start earlier and extend later into the autumn.

INVESTING IN THE SUN

In the development of many innovative technologies with consumer markets, there are four distinct phases. First, there is a great burst of enthusiasm: the numerous start-up companies find ready customers for their hastily fabricated products. After several years, the initial euphoria begins to wear off as many of these products begin to fail. The second phase, which is a period of retrenchment, then begins: customers are disillusioned, often not just with the products, but with the entire technology. Many companies fail and others cut back.

The third phase is a period of intense research and development. Those few firms that have survived start doing the kind of research and development they should have done in the first place, and, in a few years, have improved products ready for market.

The infant industry now has the task of convincing the public that *these* products will hold up and perform effectively. This period of introducing the improved technology and watching it perform is the fourth phase. Whether there is a fifth phase—that of a successful industry—depends, of course, on whether the technology proves itself in the fourth phase.

Solar heating, wind power, and some other renewables are now well into the fourth phase of their existence. After the first burst of enthusiasm in the 1970s, the 1980s saw a period of disillusionment and retrenchment. Now, in the 1990s, a new generation of renewable energy products is springing up everywhere—and these look like winners: they are durable, efficient, and increasingly cost-effective.

For investors, this means a growing number of highly promising energy firms to choose from. Because these companies are young and small, they need to be carefully researched. But, in a field that is now beginning to expand so rapidly, astute investors should see their capital expand with it.

This field is not for the buy-and-sell speculator, but for the long-term investor. Renewable energy companies are going to grow, but investors should be prepared to hold on to their stocks over a period of years. We will discuss this further in chapter 14.

SOLAR COMPANIES

Photocomm, Inc. (PCOM, NASDAQ)
602-948-8003

Next time you use your cellular phone on a stretch of road far from any city, you can think of a company called

Photocomm. Photocomm has developed a photovoltaic unit that provides electricity for what are called "cellular repeater sites." These sites are transmitters that strengthen the radio signals between cities.

This small, Arizona-based firm constructs PV arrays for many different markets. The army uses a Photocomm lightweight solar battery charger for field applications and a remote navy base uses a Photocomm power plant. The company has begun to market such diverse products as solar golf carts, pipeline leak-detection devices, and lightning-detection devices.

Photocomm also markets large PV arrays for homes or recreational vehicles. In the last few years, however, the company has been focusing on specialized systems for industrial and commercial markets.

Communications applications are a major part of the company's business right now. The same cellular companies that Photocomm works with in the U.S. are also busy developing phone networks in Latin America. The need for solar is much greater in most of these countries because the utility grid system is not so widespread.

Photocomm will design, engineer, and install specialized PV systems for almost any purpose. The company has recently been selling charging systems to geophysical exploration teams looking for oil, gas, or water. The PV modules charge batteries for the teams' complex data acquisition systems.

This is a small company that has found a very profitable niche in the growing photovoltaics industry. Revenues have risen steadily; in 1995, they rose dramatically.

Other Companies

There are several companies that have solar as an important segment of their activities. Nevada Energy and New

World Power, for example, are profiled in chapter 5. Real Goods, which markets solar products, is the subject of much of chapter 10.

There are also some large companies that are actively engaged in solar. One of these is the giant German corporation Siemens. Right now, because solar makes up only a small part of their business, Siemens cannot be considered an environmental investment. But keep an eye on it—and on other companies that get involved in solar. The field is growing so fast that there will soon be many firms engaged in all different aspects of harnessing the sun.

CHAPTER 5

SUN POWER, EARTH POWER, MOON POWER

I n the last chapter, we looked at the many uses of
direct solar power; in this chapter we're going to discuss other forms of renewable energy. The Cosmic
Power and Light Company is very diversified, as you will
see. Later in the chapter, we'll discuss how to invest in
this company, or at least in a few of its earthly sub-
sidiaries. But first, let's take a more detailed look at the
different kinds of renewable power.

Renewable energy means just that: after you use it,
there's always more. Whereas supplies of coal and oil will
run out sometime in the next century (at the present rate
of usage), the sun, which supplies most of our renewable
power, is apparently good for a few billion years. A few
pages from here, we'll look at some other reasons why
we need to start phasing out fossil fuels.

We can use the sun's energy either directly or indi-
rectly. Solar heating and photovoltaics use the sun's heat

and light directly. As for the sun's indirect mode, wind is produced by temperature differentials in the atmosphere (caused by the sun), and hydropower depends on the cycle of evaporation and rainfall. Wood and other biofuels depend on photosynthesis, which, in turn, depends on sunlight.

Geothermal energy, however, comes from the earth's internal heat. Drill down a couple of thousand meters and you have enough heat to create steam, which can run a turbine-powered generator. This is "earth power."

Maybe you thought we were kidding when we placed "moon power" in the title of this chapter. But, in certain ocean bays, the tides rise and fall to such extremes that it's possible to run turbines from the water entering and exiting the bays. The electricity generated from these water turbines can be termed "moon power" since the gravitational pull of the moon helps to cause the tides (gravitation from the sun also plays a part). Moon power is presently not widely used, but it is a renewable form of energy with some promise.

EARTH POWER

Most forms of direct solar power are eminently practical for home use, as well as large-scale power generation. The same is true of wind power; there are large wind generators and very small ones.

In the case of a few renewable sources, however, large-scale development is the only practical option. Geothermal power, for example, requires the kind of capital and technology that only a corporation is capable of.

The inside of the earth is hot. Every thirty meters down into the earth's crust, the temperature increases by 1°C. In certain geologically active areas, this heat is much closer to the surface; geothermal plants are usually located in such areas.

To tap the heat, holes are drilled several thousand feet into the earth. Water is pumped down through pipes and heated up to well above boiling. As steam, it is returned to the surface and used to run a turbine, which turns an electric generator. The hot water and steam is then circulated back into the earth to be reheated.

Geothermal is one of the most cost-effective of the the renewables. Once the wells are dug and the infrastructure is in place, power can often be generated at less cost than from fossil fuel plants. Geothermal plants are now operating in 27 different countries, producing 50 million megawatts of power each year.

AIR POWER

Getting power from moving air is an ancient technology. Windmills have been pumping water and grinding grain for 2,000 years. Producing electricity is a relatively new use, but one that is rapidly being employed all over the world.

In the 1930s, a few companies began to produce small windmills that ran electric generators. Before the Rural Electrification Administration brought utility power to the rural areas of the U.S., thousands of farms, especially on the windy Great Plains, had "home light plants."

With the explosion of interest in renewable technologies in the 1970s, this technology was updated. A great variety of small wind turbines, some well-constructed, some not, appeared in the space of a few years and found a ready market with back-to-the-land homesteaders.

The variety may have decreased by the 1990s, but the power output and reliability of the new, small wind machines has made them much more effective. Modern wind turbines have two- or three-bladed rotors resembling aircraft propellors and are mounted on towers 40 to 120 feet high. An electric generator mounted behind the rotors is powered by the rotors as they are turned by the wind.

Size and cost vary, but with batteries for storage, these machines produce enough electricity for modest household use. It's necessary, of course, to live in an area windy enough to power the turbine; a minimum average wind speed of 10 miles per hour is desirable. Because of the variability of the wind, many people combine the turbines with other sources of power to keep the batteries charged.

Photovoltaic systems can act as an excellent complement to wind power because in winter, when there is less sunlight, there is usually more wind. These hybrid systems often include small gasoline generators as backups, but studies have shown that these are rarely used. A well-planned system can get almost all of its power from wind and sun.

The market for these wind "micro-turbines" is growing rapidly, but the major action these days is in the area of macro wind projects. These involve large arrays of giant wind turbines—called "wind farms"—producing power for electrical utility grids. Like the smaller wind machines, the larger ones have also gone through a sorting-out process since the 1970s.

Encouraged by the generous tax credits offered to producers of renewable energy in the mid-1970s, a few companies built large-scale wind projects. New regulations required utilities to buy power from renewable sources, so there was a ready market for the electricity produced.

Exciting as the prospects seemed, however, the early technology was not really up to the job. Machines failed with regularity, and, once the tax credits were phased out, the price of the power produced was not competitive with coal- or natural gas–fired plants.

This picture has changed radically in the last 20 years. There is presently a worldwide boom in extracting power from the wind. On every continent, wind turbines are generating electricity. These new turbines are state-of-the-art machines with aerodynamic blades made of synthetics, advanced electronic controls, and excellent reliability. Power produced has risen from 100 kilowatts per machine to 300–750 kilowatts.

Because power production and efficiency are on the way up, costs are on the way down. Wind developers have recently signed contracts to deliver electricity at 4 to 5 cents per kilowatt/hour. These prices mean that wind power can now compete in the marketplace with fossil-fueled generating plants.

HYDROPOWER

Most forms of renewable energy lend themselves both to large- and small-scale power production. Hydropower, for example, brings to mind the Grand Coulee Dam or other immense hydroelectric projects. But so-called "micro-hydro" units are relatively cheap as a source of power for an individual homestead or village; all you need is a nearby stream.

The Real Goods *Solar Living Sourcebook* (see chapter 10) tells how to install a micro-hydro system in a small stream and also relates some of the advantages of these units. The cost, for example, can be much less than other renewable systems such as photovoltaics. The amount of power produced is usually substantial, and, because the flow is continuous, only a small battery storage is needed for occasional power surges.

Of course, you do need a good year-round stream. But small, home-based hydropower systems are increasing in this country and abroad. Medium-sized projects built by independent power producers are also growing in number. When properly constructed, the environmental impact of these projects is minimal, the power is clean and nonpolluting, and, once the turbines are in place, the cost of the power is extremely low.

In the case of large hydro projects, the power is also clean and cheap, but it usually comes at great cost to the surrounding environment. Giant dams, constructed at tremendous cost, flood large areas of land. In fact, solar facilities could generate the same amount of power as a hydropower plant on much less land. In addition, changing a river into a lake alters the plant and animal life in the entire ecosystem.

In the U.S., most sites for large hydro facilities have already been exploited. In less developed countries, however, such projects are seen as a cheap way to generate electricity. In Malaysia, for example, $5.8 billion is being spent on the 2,400 megawatt Bakun Dam. This dam will inundate 170,000 acres and require the clearing of 200,000 acres of forest for power lines. Tribal people will have to be relocated, and a large part of the ecosystem will be irrevocably changed.

Giant hydro projects used to seem attractive when compared to coal and nuclear generating plants. Nowadays, however, there are better ways of producing clean power with a low impact on the ecosystem. Nevertheless, well-planned medium and small hydro projects remain environmentally sound. One of the companies profiled at the end of this chapter has invested in several such facilities. Investors can watch for other, similar firms.

POWER FROM THE OCEAN

Usable power from the oceans comes in three forms: tidal, wave, and thermal. Of these, the first two look very promising.

Tidal power is another ancient form of energy. As early as the eleventh century, tide mills were operating on the coasts of Spain, France, and England. Water flowed through a sluice into a storage pond with the incoming tide; when the tide reversed, the water would flow back into the sea turning a water wheel as it left the pond.

The modern use of tidal energy involves a dam, called a barrage, built across an estuary. The water flows into the estuary through sluices at high tide; on its way out at low tide, the water turns turbine generators.

Several experimental tidal barrage generators have been constructed and the results have been encouraging. An operation at La Rance, in northern France, presently produces 250 megawatts. Larger commercial projects are now planned in almost every country with a suitable coastline, particularly France, the United Kingdom, Canada, and Russia.

The impact on the marine life and the ecosystems around the barriers is being studied carefully. Although each site is different, no serious effects have been noticed as yet. The visual impact of a large dam built across an inlet is, of course, a consideration, and the barrier might also be a problem for shipping.

Another difficulty with the tidal barrages is the large amount of capital necessary to build the facilities. Successful development will depend partly on the cost of capital and the price of fossil fuels.

The up-and-down motion of the waves is another ocean power source that is beginning to be utilized. This technology is still in its early stages, with several different experimental systems in the running. Some recent advances, however, make wave power look very promising for certain applications.

A strange-looking barge sits in the Shannon River estuary in Ireland. It consists of a central barge with two longer, flat platforms extending on either side. These two platforms are hinged to the central barge; as they rise and fall with the waves, their motion drives pumps inside the central barge, just as a handle drives an old-fashioned hand pump. The central barge is stabilized by a large, flat steel plate suspended in the water 26 feet below; this stability raises efficiency by allowing the "pump handles" to push against the immovable central barge.

This prototype, called the McCabe Wave Pump, has been developed by Peter McCabe, President and Chief Engineer of Hydam Technology, Ltd., of Ireland, and Michael McCormick of the Department of Engineering at Johns Hopkins University. It is designed to pump seawater to a desalinization plant onshore. A commercial unit would replace pumps powered by oil, forcing the salty ocean water first through a filtering system and then through a reverse-osmosis desalinization system, producing potable water. However, the same wave motion that drives pumps could also power electric generators; this technology will be the subject of future studies.

Why is this significant? It's significant because there are 100,000 populated islands around the world, most of which are in need of both potable water and electricity. Coastal regions, especially in developing countries, could also benefit. Water from desalinization plants is expensive because the energy to run the plants is expensive. Electricity is also expensive in island communities.

The projected costs of potable water produced by the wave pump could be as low as $7.00 per 1,000 gallons; electricity costs are estimated at 12 cents a kilowatt hour. Both of these figures would represent significant savings for most islands and many coastal regions.

Commercial application of wave power is still several years off. Much more testing with various prototypes is necessary. But the possibilities for this renewable technology look very exciting.

Most steam engines run at very high temperatures (950°F to 1,000°F). because their efficiency goes up with the difference between the vaporizing and condensing temperatures. It is possible to run a vapor engine at a temperature differential of as little as 36°F. This is the basis of ocean thermal energy conversion, or OTEC.

In the tropics, temperatures at the surface of the oceans are often as high as 77°F, while the water 3,000 feet down is only 41°F. A gas that vaporizes at low temperatures (such as the refrigerant, Freon) is heated by the surface waters; the resulting vapor powers an engine and then is condensed by the cold, deep waters, which have been pumped to the surface. Because the efficiencies are so low with this small temperature differential (about 2.5 percent), thousands of gallons of deep water are required to produce useable amounts of power.

This means a very large floating power plant; a 100 megawatt plant would have a displacement of at least 200,000 tons. Moving tremendous quantities of cold water to the surface could have significant effects on the environment, from the marine ecosystem to local weather patterns. Various experimental OTEC plants have been built, but right now the costs are too high for commercial applications.

At the present, tidal power and wave power appear to be the most likely candidates for energy from the ocean. For investors, the smaller scale of the wave power systems means that new companies might be created to build and install them. This will be a few years down the road, but keep your eyes open.

Biomass

The term "biomass" covers all organic matter used for fuel (called biofuel). This ranges from plants specifically raised for fuel to organic waste of all kinds including agricultural, industrial, and food wastes as well as sewage. Biomass, in the form of firewood, supplied 90 percent of the energy needs in the U.S. until the mid-nineteenth century. Wood still supplies almost 40 percent of the fuel in developing countries.

Since the 1970s, there has been a resurgence of interest in wood as a fuel in the U.S. This has caused some problems; wood, as burned in most stoves and fire-places, is a highly polluting fuel. During the winter, many communities find themselves immersed in a sooty haze; some have had to ban wood burning on days when climatic conditions keep the smoke close to the ground.

All this smoke stems from the fact that old-fashioned woodstoves burn at only about 50 percent efficiency. Twenty-five percent of the wood remains as ash, and 20 percent to 30 percent escapes up the chimney as unburned hydrocarbons, creosote, and other toxins. Modern woodstoves, due to controls as stringent as those for automobiles, produce much less pollution. And wood-chip gasifiers, designed to heat large buildings or produce electricity, are even more efficient; they leave only 1 percent ash and almost no hydrocarbons or creosote.

In a gasifier, such high temperatures are created that the wood, or other biofuel, is turned into a gas before it burns. This is why combustion is so efficient and low-polluting. There are now 350 small gasifier power plants

Carbon Dioxide Buildup

Why does burning biomass not cause carbon dioxide buildup while burning fossil fuels does? This is because oil, coal, and natural gas are stored biomass, created from organic matter millions of years ago. Burning these fuels releases the stored carbon dioxide into the atmosphere.

Plant biomass, on the other hand, fixes (absorbs) carbon dioxide from the atmosphere while it is growing, then releases the same amount when burned. If it wasn't burned, plant biomass would release the carbon dioxide in any case when it decayed. Biomass, then, remains part of the natural carbon dioxide cycle whether it is burned or left to decay.

operating in the U.S.; these utilize a variety of fuels, from wood chips to agricultural by-products.

Technologies abound that use plants as a fuel source. We have made methanol in this country from corn and other products for a long time. Methanol and ethanol are both excellent fuels for internal combustion engines; they even produce somewhat less of certain kinds of pollution than gasoline.

In 1975, Brazil started a crash program to replace much of its expensive, imported oil with domestically produced ethanol. By 1987, ethanol accounted for 18 percent of fuel for transportation. Most of this was made from the fermentation of sugarcane juice.

In this process, the remaining biomass from the cane—*bagasse*—and the waste water—*vinasse*—are simply thrown away or burned. A new process called anaerobic digestion can greatly increase the efficiency of ethanol production by making methane from the bagasse and vinasse. The methane can be used to power the ethanol distillery. When compressed, this biofuel can also be a replacement for diesel fuel in trucks and other vehicles.

The anaerobic process utilizes bacteria that live in oxygen-free environments. These bacteria feed on the waste and produce methane gas in the process. Methane is a flammable gas with properties similar to natural gas.

Anaerobic digestion can be used with almost any biomass to produce methane. It is presently being employed at some sewage plants in the U.S. After methane is produced, the remaining sludge is processed into fertilizer.

Methane—or "biogas," as it is often called—is an especially promising fuel for agricultural areas in developing countries. In India and China, small anaerobic digesters produce biogas for farms and communities. Animal manure and human waste usually provide the fuel for the generators.

The gas powers generators to make electricity for villages; in many cases, this is the first power that the villagers have ever had. And, in many of these operations, the heat of the anaerobic process sterilizes the wastes so that they may be used as fertilizer.

Biomass: Pros and Cons

Biomass looks very promising in many applications, particularly when the fuel is agricultural by-products or other waste. When the crops are grown on land that might otherwise be used for food production, however, the technology looks much less attractive, particularly in developing countries. In these cases, one has to ask if other kinds of renewables, such as solar or wind, wouldn't be more appropriate.

Let's look at a list of pros and cons for biomass, keeping in mind that the technologies vary quite a bit.

Advantages:

In many areas, especially in developing countries, the jobs that biomass technology provides are highly valued.

Biofuels can be residues from food crops, which would otherwise be destroyed.

Biofuels are a renewable source of energy; they can replace fossil fuel generators in many areas.

When modern technology is employed, such as gasifiers or anaerobic digesters, biomass is a much less polluting fuel than coal or oil.

Excess carbon dioxide is not produced (see previous explanation).

Certain technologies, such as biogas production from manure or human waste, provide electricity and fertilizer for villages in developing agricultural areas.

Disadvantages:

Plants grown for fuel take up land that could be used for food production.

Plants are a middleman in energy production. In many cases, it might be more cost effective to build solar generators and produce electricity directly from the sun.

Growing biomass is often water-intensive agriculture.

Gasifiers generally operate at low efficiencies (14 percent to 18 percent compared to 35 percent to 40 percent for large power plants).

Biofuels still produce some pollution when they burn, even in gasifiers and new woodstoves.

It requires energy and labor to grow biomass. Other renewables need much less human energy to operate once they are in place. Does biomass cultivation take labor and skills away from other needed tasks?

Solar and wind generators can be placed in desert or other land areas that are unsuitable for crops or habitation. In many areas, animals can graze around solar or wind machines. Biomass, on the other hand, requires good agricultural land.

Investors need to know about these technologies because some independent power producers (such as Nevada Energy, profiled later in this chapter) are already beginning to use them. We are going to see a lot more of biomass technology in the coming years, in all its many forms.

WHAT'S WRONG WITH BUSINESS AS USUAL?

What we're aiming for, of course, is the eventual replacement of as much fossil fuel and nuclear power as possible with renewable sources. This is going to take a few decades, and the statistics following show why. The economies of the industrialized countries presently run almost entirely on oil, coal, natural gas, nuclear power, and hydropower. The developing world still uses a good deal of biofuel, especially wood, but is moving toward dependence on fossil fuels.

The tables following give an idea of what we have to contend with.

Let's make a brief summary of the drawbacks of fossil fuels and nuclear power. Why do we want to replace fossil fuels and nuclear power with renewable sources?

Smog from petroleum products and coal and acid rain from coal are two good reasons to start with. Next come the billions of dollars the U.S. pays for foreign oil— a major contributor to our negative trade balance.

TABLE 5.1 Energy Sources

	U.S. Energy Sources	World Energy Sources
Petroleum	40%	34%
Coal	23%	24%
Natural Gas	22%	17%
Nuclear	5%	4%
Hydro	5%	5%
Biomass (mostly wood)	4%	15%
Renewable	less than 1%	1%

Nuclear power has proven to be an expensive dead-end street; accidents which release radioactivity, such as the one at Three Mile Island, are always a danger, and there is no safe way to dispose of the deadly wastes.

Natural gas is a much more benign fuel; it produces little pollution, although it, along with the other fossil fuels, produces carbon dioxide. While some climatologists are doubtful that the earth is undergoing a warming trend, the majority not only believe that it is, but that carbon dioxide released by burning fossil fuels is the culprit. Planetary warming is not something we want: it means vanishing forests, growing deserts, and the inundation of coastal cities, along with the possibility of other, even worse, consequences.

Finally, another excellent reason for shifting to renewables is that fossil fuels are disappearing

TABLE 5.2 End Use of Energy in the U.S.

End Use	Percentage of Total
Electricity Generation	36%
Transportation	28%
Industrial and Miscellaneous	22%
Residential and Commercial	14%

commodities. At present rates of consumption, we will run out of oil before the middle of the next century, and natural gas not long after. We have lots of coal reserves, but if these are used to replace the lost oil and gas, we will run out of coal, too, before the year 2100.

Renewable energy sources, on the other hand, are safe, non-polluting or low-polluting, they don't contribute to carbon dioxide buildup, they are cheaper once their infrastructure is in place, and they are not going to run out anytime soon. With advantages like these, it's pretty clear that renewables are our future and that the sooner we start using them, the better off we will be.

COSTS

How quickly we make the shift to renewable power sources depends to a great extent on its cost. Electricity production, which uses about 36 percent of the total energy in the U.S., is one area where renewables are beginning to be competitive.

The cost of electricity varies widely across the country. The price per kilowatt hour ranges from 4 cents to as much as 20 cents with an average of about 10 cents per kWh. You will find what you pay per kWh on your utility bill. The price of electricity is important because renewable energy must compete with power generated by oil, nuclear, coal, or natural gas–fired turbines. Whether a renewable will be competitive depends not only on how cheaply it can be produced, but on the price of electricity in the various regions of the country.

Utility-sized photovoltaic electricity costs about 25 cents per kWh at present; in 1994, the U.S. Department of Energy estimated that PV power will fall to 12 cents to 20 cents per kWh before the year 2000. This estimate is already out-of-date, however. As we saw in the last chapter, utilizing brand-new technology, several major corporations have plans to market PV power for as little as 5.5 cents per kWh.

Wind power is already being sold at prices competitive with fossil fuel generators and may underprice them in a few years.

Utilities have recently become very interested in clean energy because Phase I of the Clean Air Act Amendments went into effect in January 1995. Phase II of the Act, with even more strict requirements, will take effect in 1998. Utilities are, therefore, looking for dependable sources of clean power to meet any increase in demand. This increase in use will help lower costs of renewables over the long run.

Electricity generation, of course, is just one use of energy. In order to phase out fuels which pollute, we will also have to replace them with renewables in the other three categories in Table 5.2. In succeeding chapters, we will deal with ways of introducing renewables into transportation and industry. The use of solar energy for home power has been covered in the last chapter, and we will discuss other ways renewables can be incorporated into the home in chapters 10 and 11.

TWENTY-FIRST CENTURY THINKING

In chapter 1, we spoke of the new kind of thinking necessary to fully understand the changes inherent in the new technologies. The idea of scarcity—of only so much to go around—is one of the modes of thinking that must give way to the new mode of abundance in the next century.

Renewable power is a perfect example of abundance. The sun bombards us every day with much more energy than we can possibly use. As our ability to utilize renewable power grows, the many different kinds of renewables will constitute an embarrassment of riches.

Companies

Independent power producers—companies that produce electricity and sell it to utilities—are some of the most promising prospects for investors. There is a small, but growing, number of these firms specializing in renewable power sources. The companies portrayed following are two of the best. Electricity from solar, wind, hydro, and geothermal power is being sold right now, but watch for other companies in any of the technologies described in this chapter and chapter 4.

Suppliers of products for the power producers, industry, and consumers will also be companies to watch. Photocomm is one of these; retail firms such as Real Goods should also do well (see chapter 10).

The New World Power Corporation *(NWPC, NASDAQ) 203-435-4000*

Companies that position themselves early in the field of alternate energy have a good possibility of growing into major corporations during the first years of the twenty-first century. New World Power is one such firm.

This company has three strategies: first, to sell electricity from renewable sources to utilities; second, to provide wireless power for remote areas; and, third, to market renewable power systems to remote villages.

New World presently has six operating wind farms and twelve more scheduled to start producing power in 1995 or 1996. The company also has several hydroelectric plants on-line as well as a 40 percent interest in a Chinese hydro project due to be completed in late 1995. The wind farms, which are located in Europe, Latin America, and the U.S., will produce roughly 250 megawatts of power altogether.

When it comes to wireless power for remote areas, New World depends on Photocomm (profiled in the last chapter). Photocomm provides wireless power for remote scientific locations and military applications as well as PV arrays for remote villages. New World owns 51 percent of Photocomm stock.

Photovoltaics is only one of the segments of the systems designed for remote villages. Thousands of small villages, especially in the developing world, either have no electric power or depend on expensive diesel generators. The cost to run utility lines through jungles and up mountains is often too steep. New World will design a power system for a village based on the best combination of available resources: wind, solar, or hydro energy with diesel generators used only for backup. The company plans to focus its village projects on Latin America and the Caribbean.

The company is still in the development stage. But as the various wind and hydro projects come on-line in 1995 and 1996, New World will see a significant jump in revenues.

Nevada Energy Company
(NNRGA, NASDAQ NATIONAL MARKET)
702-786-7679

Started in 1982 as a developer of geothermal energy, Nevada Energy is a survivor of the great shakeout of the 1980s, when young energy companies, stripped of their tax advantages, dropped like autumn leaves.

In 1988, Nevada Energy underwent a hostile take-over by a corporate raider and went into chapter 11 bankruptcy the same year. The present managers then acquired a majority interest and, during the next two years, reorganized the company and restructured the debt. When the firm emerged from bankruptcy in 1991, creditors were paid off at 100 cents on the dollar and long-term debt was almost eliminated.

Nevada Energy has now become a player in the growing market for clean energy. In 1994, the company purchased a 50.01 percent interest in the Smith Project, which consists of 77 wind turbines in the San Gorgonio Pass near Palm Springs, California. These turbines were originally built at a cost of $18 million, but because of their poor condition, Nevada Energy was able to purchase its interest for only $500,000 in cash and stock.

Interestingly enough, the firm that bought the other 49.09 percent interest in the Smith Project is the New World Power Corporation. Nevada Energy has formed a joint venture with New World Power to upgrade and further develop the wind power site. Now called the San Jacinto Power Company, the wind farm has a generating capacity of 8 megawatts and the company plans to add facilities generating another 10 megawatts. San Jacinto Power has a 20-year purchase agreement for this electricity with Southern California Edison.

Nevada Energy also recently puchased a geothermal plant in Yerington, Nevada. The company plans to upgrade the power production, which has operated at only 48 percent of capacity. In the meantime, with the purchase came two 30-year power sales contracts for 1.47 megawatts with Sierra Pacific Power Company.

Nevada Energy is covering all possibilities in the energy field. In addition to wind and geothermal, the company is pursuing an innovative type of ethanol production from biomass. This technology eliminates several steps in the production of ethanol and allows for the use of low-cost biomass materials, such as sawdust, waste paper, and alfalfa.

In the Caribbean, the company is investigating the possibility of using bagasse, a by-product of sugarcane processing, to produce ethanol. A pilot wind power plant is also planned for the Caribbean.

Nevada Energy has a sound business plan, based on diversity of energy production in the renewable energy field. The strategy is to purchase distressed facilities at low prices and to upgrade their power production. At the same time, the managers work closely with utilities to make sure they will have a market for the increased electricity production.

The company also works to optimize the present tax advantages for renewable energy. Such benefits as energy production credits for wind power plants, energy tax credits, and five-year accelerated depreciation can greatly reduce taxes or shelter pre-tax income.

The long-term power contracts with utilities give the company a steady source of income, which makes for a solid base from which to expand into different areas.

CHAPTER 6

RECYCLING:
THE HARD STUFF

*waste   n. superfluous, used or unwanted
material (archaic)*
> —*WEBSTER'S INTERNATIONAL DICTIONARY.
> COPYRIGHT 2050.*

NO MORE WASTE

Sustainable development often requires a change in our thinking. For example, when you look at used products of any kind, do you think "waste," or do you think "resources"? A growing number of businesses are thinking resources. This trend means that by the year 2050, our present idea of waste will probably be an antiquated concept.

In this chapter, we're going to view how this shift in consciousness is manifesting itself in the world. We're going to discuss recycling in its various forms and see how it makes economic as well as environmental sense. From cottage industries to larger, publicly owned companies, the opportunities for entrepreneurs in this new field are seemingly endless. We'll take a look at a few of these firms and at their prospects for success.

NO MORE DUMPS

Since the beginning of human history, people have discarded unwanted materials, often in piles, which have proved invaluable to archaeologists. Future archaeological researchers investigating the societies of 2050 will have to depend on other sources, however, because by the middle of the next century, dumps and landfills, as we know them, will be a thing of the past. This disappearing act is already happening; in this country, the number of landfills has shrunk from 30,000 in 1978 to fewer than 5,000 today.

Our industrial civilization can no longer tolerate the loss of raw materials and the pollution inherent in the throwaway system of waste disposal. Over the coming decades, manufactured goods will increasingly be reused or recycled; the firms producing the goods will also take responsibilty for their recycling. In Europe, this is already beginning to happen.

Recycling makes obvious economic sense. A great deal of time, material, energy, and skill goes into fabricating the products we use. If we simply throw them out when they're no longer useful, we lose all this precious input.

The idea of recycling and reuse is to recapture as much as possible of this input. There are essentially two ways of doing this. One is to break down the materials into basic components. A few companies are doing this with used tires; the tires are chemically reduced to carbon black, steel, and oil, all of which can be sold on the open market.

The other way is to use the finished product in another form. For example, there are several cottage industries that cut up tires for use as shoe soles or other products. Wood and plastic products are also being re-formed into new shapes and put to new uses.

Recycling makes sense for the ecosystem as well as the economy. The trouble with throwing away complex manufactured goods is that nature doesn't know what to do with them. The natural world has perfected the recycling of organic materials, but these artificial products just don't break down as organic things do. Or, if they do break down, they often release toxic chemicals into the ecosystem.

Recycling our manufactured goods is our job. We can't depend on nature to do it for us.

In this next section, we're going to look at the kind of recycling most of us are familiar with on an everyday basis, that is, the recycling of materials such as glass, paper, and aluminum.

REDUCE, REUSE, RECYCLE

A few facts and figures: in the U.S., cities and towns with curbside recycling numbered 7,200 in 1994, up from 1,000 in 1988. Of U.S. households, 41 percent are served by these programs and many more are served by multi-family programs and drop-off sites. Eighty-four percent of residents in communities where recycling is mandated favor these laws, 66 percent favor such laws in towns where recycling is not required.

There are good reasons for this growth in recycling and for the support that helps make it happen. Recycling not only lowers the cost of dealing with waste, it employs more people in the community. Recycling also can attract industries that offer high-paying industrial jobs.

Of course, going into the recycling business means that communities are subject to market conditions for the recycled materials. Prices tend to rise and fall with market demand and industry's ability to deal with it. Prices tend to rise and fall with demand, which is connected to industry's ability to use recycled materials. During the 1980s, demand fell off for many recycled products because, while the supply increased, industries were set up to deal mostly with virgin raw materials.

Many states then enacted laws mandating that a certain minimum of materials must come from recycled sources. These laws, coupled with the realization by producers that used materials are often cheaper than new, have led to the construction of large new facilities to handle recyclables. As a result in 1994 and 1995, prices for paper, aluminum, and plastic bottles were near all-time highs.

So, when manufacturers can handle the used materials, communities receive good prices for their recyclables. But how about the industries that actually fabricate the new products—does recycling benefit them? Let's look at a few more facts and figures.

One ton of recycled paper can be manufactured with 64 percent less energy and 58 percent less water than are used for paper from wood pulp. Seventeen trees are saved and air pollution is reduced by 34 percent. Manufacturing new glass from recycled glass needs only 65 percent of the energy of starting from scratch. And aluminum? Well, aluminum made from your used pet-food cans requires just *one-tenth* as much energy as starting from bauxite ore.

So industry benefits, the utilities benefit because they don't have to build new generating facilities for these energy-intensive industries, and we all benefit from stable prices for new products. The environment is helped by the burning of less fossil fuel and reduced mining and lumbering. And last, but not least, natural resources are saved.

THE ENVIRONMENTAL PLASTICS INDUSTRY

Environmental plastics—sounds like an oxymoron, doesn't it? But the idea behind this new industry is to keep plastics out of the waste stream. No matter what you may have heard, plastics are *not* biodegradable, but are often toxic to the ecosystem when thrown away. When recycled, however, plastics can be put to myriad uses; entrepreneurs have let their imaginations run wild, and the result is the flowering of a new industry.

These recyclers include not just plastics, but wood, metal, tires, and glass, too. Here are some of the recycled products as cataloged by the *Real Goods Solar Living Source Book:*

> There are framing systems [for buildings] made out of recycled styrofoam cups and steel, recycled plastic lumber . . . and pressed scrap wood beams. Siding and shingles made from composites like shredded newspaper, cardboard, plastic, tires, bottles, and cement often have better thermal and maintenance performance than traditional materials. You can find carpet and floor coverings made from recycled plastic jugs, and tiles made from scrap brick pieces, automobile glass, and bottles.

These products reuse the materials by shredding or reshaping them. But there are also a number of companies that chemically break down the plastics and sell the recycled materials to plastics manufacturers. Other firms make a business out of fabricating their products only from recycled plastics; their materials cost is less and there is a ready market to environmentally conscious consumers.

Recycled Houses

High on a hill overlooking San Francisco Bay a new kind of house is under construction. When completed, it won't look that different from other houses, but there are big differences in the materials and construction. For one thing, even though people are hard at work, there is an eerie silence for a construction site: no power saws or noisy hammering. The materials for the walls are being cut and *glued* together.

These materials are large boards made from 90 percent recycled styrofoam and 10 percent portland cement. Fabricated by Integrid Building Systems of Berkeley, California, the boards are inexpensive, strong, easy to work with, and highly insulating. This is one of the construction materials of tomorrow.

RECYCLING THE BIG STUFF

There are currently 500 million major household appliances in use in the United States. Refrigerators, freezers, stoves, washers, dryers, dishwashers, furnaces, and water heaters all provide services we have come to depend on. When they need to be replaced, however, they become a major headache, not only because of their sheer bulk, but because most of them contain toxic substances.

In 1990, 32 million of these appliances were junked, and this figure will grow to 54 million by the year 2000. This is a lot of trash, and disposing of it has become much more difficult. Many landfills ban large appliances because they take up too much space and contain hazardous materials. Federal regulations now require special handling for such materials as mercury, chlorofluorocarbons (CFCs), polychlorinated biphenyls, and sulfur dioxide, all of which are found in various appliances.

In addition to the disposal problem, many older appliances, particularly refrigerators and freezers, use electricity very inefficiently. Many utility companies have been offering incentives to customers to replace their old refrigerators with new, energy-efficient models. Some utilities will even pay customers for their old machines.

Later in the chapter, we will discuss a company that has made a business of recycling these appliances. Right now, however, let's look at how intelligent government mandates can cause changes in design that make recycling of appliances and other products much easier.

In Japan and some western European countries, manufacturers are being required to recycle many of their products. Japanese manufacturers have established resource recovery centers and are redesigning their products to include more of the recovered materials. They are also making complex products, such as appliances, much easier to disassemble.

New designs are also showing up in the European auto industry. BMW now has a separate plant to disassemble and recycle its used cars. Older Volvos are taken apart at a plant called The Environmental Car Recycling, in Sweden. And 17 industrial companies in Germany have created a firm called Automobile Recycling im Verbund, which plans to recycle all but five percent of a used car.

The types of plastics used in most autos are especially difficult to recycle because they're composed of mixed resins. But Volvo is developing new methods of remolding and reusing the plastic components in its cars. And General Motors has developed a high-temperature process for turning these composites into natural gas and fuel oil.

The direction in which the industrialized world is heading is toward the complete responsibility of a manufacturer for a product from cradle to grave. While setting up systems like this is initially costly for manufacturers, the savings will continue indefinitely.

This is a perfect example of government taking the initiative by requiring that industry change its way of doing business. With a combination of incentives and mandates, government can overcome any initial resistance. And, because all industries in a given field have to comply with the new requirements, the playing field remains level. Then, when the new methods are in place, industry will reap the benefits of recycling.

COMPANIES

Appliance Recycling Centers of America, Inc. (ARCI, NASDAQ) 612-930-9000

In this chapter, we discussed the large number of appliances that need to be disposed of. Appliance Recycling makes a business out of recycling these masses of metal and other substances. At ARCA processing centers, any hazardous substances are removed for recycling. The remaining metals—steel, copper, and aluminum—are shredded and sent to metal recovery centers.

Because older appliances use electricity so inefficiently, ARCA has been able to contract with utilities to recycle these kilowatt-eaters. The utilities provide incentives to their customers to turn in their old refrigerators, and ARCA personnel pick them up and take them to one of their centers.

This is one of the best illustrations I have seen of the win/win/win benefits of recycling. The electric consumer spends less on electricity and gets a bonus from the utility company; the utilities save by not having to build expensive power plants; the recycling company adds to the economy by employing workers, earning money, paying taxes, etc.; and last, but not least, we all benefit by having the metals and the toxic substances recycled instead of dumped into the environment.

Perhaps we should add to this list investors who see their money grow. After a promising start in 1987, ARCA has had a few difficult years. The company now seems to have stabilized, but investors should get the most current information.

Unique Tire Recycling Inc.
(UKT, VANCOUVER EXCHANGE) 604-683-5664

There are 250 million tires discarded in the U.S. every year and there are a total of 3 billion tires in waste piles all over the country. These piles not only take up valuable space, but they occasionally catch fire, sending clouds of noxious smoke into the atmosphere. In short, discarded tires have been a nuisance and an environmental problem.

Unique Tire is a perfect example of a company that sees a resource where others see only problems. The company has perfected a Hydrocarbon Thermal Processor, which reduces used tires to their component parts: oil, carbon black, and steel. All three of these materials are in demand for many industrial uses and bring good prices on the commodity markets.

The Thermal Processor has been going through extensive final testing, while still processing 100 tires an hour. The time this has taken has discouraged many investors, but this technology presents an opportunity for more patient investors. (If there is one thing environmental investors need, it is patience! New technology takes time, but the rewards can be great.)

The thermal process used for tires can be also modified to reduce plastics to their components. The company is concentrating on tires right now, but down the road, the handling of waste plastics could be a major part of its business.

In the meantime, Unique Tire has income from its TerraMat™, a product made from used truck and bus tires, which acts as a temporary road in soft terrain.

Unique Tire is presently negotiating with two British companies. This means that the Thermal Processsor may soon be in action in western Europe.

I see Unique Tire as one of the most promising of the recycling firms. There is an inexhaustible supply of raw materials, and the steel, oil, and carbon black will always find ready markets. The company's income will depend only on how fast they can build and operate the processsors. And processing the raw materials—the tires and plastics—can greatly aid the environment.

CHAPTER 7

RECYCLING:
THE SOFT STUFF

In addition to the hard goods, there will always be soft organic waste composed of food from homes and restaurants and by-products from farms and industry. Add municipal sewage to this, and you have a yearly figure of 100 million tons of organic waste in North America alone. In order to deal with this impressive quantity of waste, every community needs to have its own composting plant, which will turn biodegradable waste into useful products. These end products may then be sold, providing money to run the plant.

In the year 2050, an aerial view of a community will reveal no messy dumps or landfills polluting the air, soil, and groundwater. Instead, in the industrial section of town, you will see garbage trucks unloading waste materials at one end of a large building. Sewage lines also terminate at this building.

At the other end of this structure, trucks are loading the finished products from this recycling plant: ingredients for animal feed, made from food waste, and high-quality organic fertilizer, made from sewage sludge and the rest of the garbage.

The high heat inherent in the composting process purifies the waste, killing all disease-producing microorganisms. The process is quiet, almost odorless, and produces no harmful materials as side effects.

This is not just a futuristic fantasy. Like most twenty-first century projections in this book, the process described is being utilized right now by a few forward-looking firms. And none too soon: we need recycling systems like these very badly.

Organic waste, which comprises 30 percent of all solid waste, is one of the worst polluters. In landfills, the decomposing materials, including disease-producing bacteria, leach into the soil and eventually into the groundwater. The methane gas produced by the uncontrolled composting is a fire hazard, and the unpleasant odors are obvious to anyone living nearby.

In order to prevent problems like these, government regulations have begun to limit what goes into landfills. These regulations, added to the fact that many landfills have reached their capacity, have drastically reduced the number of such facilities.

UP IN SMOKE

People concerned about the environment are often confused by conflicting information. Investors, in particular, can be confused by information sent by companies they are investigating. While many firms call their products and processes "environmental," a closer look reveals just the opposite.

A case in point is incinerators. Incineration of waste products is often touted as a "green" solution, especially when the heat is used to run a turbine that generates electricity for the local utility company. Burning things up has the appeal of seeming to get rid of waste by turning it into vapor and using the heat for useful purposes.

This is a fantasy, unfortunately, and a damaging one at that. The "vapor" produced is actually toxic smoke, full of poisonous compounds. Much of this is caught by pollution devices—scrubbers and baghouses—but this means that these toxins are mixed into the remaining ash. This fly ash is what remains after the burning; 30 tons of it are produced for every 100 tons of household waste.

Incineration, then, not only pollutes the air, it doesn't even get rid of the waste. It reduces the volume that goes to the landfill, but it also concentrates the toxins. Heavy metals such as lead, mercury, and cadmium do not degrade; they must be kept out of the soil and water indefinitely. The plastic liners in most landfills, however, are guaranteed for just twenty years, thereafter the toxins can—and, almost certainly will—leach into the soil.

Communities pay heavily for the right to have an incinerator pollute their environment. Municipal bonds usually furnish the capital to build the facilities, and the town must provide a landfill for the fly ash. The town also pays the company operating the incinerator tipping fees to accept the waste and even guarantees that a certain amount of garbage will be delivered. Utilities are required to buy any electricity generated at a high fixed price.

With these guarantees in place, profits are also guaranteed, which is why incineration has become such big business. Profits also mean more money for public relations, which is why you may have heard favorable things about incineration.

States and communities that opt for recycling and some sort of composting do much better financially. A study by two M.I.T. researchers found that the state of Massachusetts could have saved more than $200 per ton of waste, had it chosen to emphasize recycling instead of incineration.

Incinerators destroy raw materials so the fine products we discussed in the last chapter and in this one never see the light of day. And all the time and energy spent in fabricating the original products goes up in smoke.

In chapter 13 we will look at new methods of destroying waste with heat. A few of these procedures look promising, but they are very different from normal incinerators. Similarly, the carefully designed low-pollution turbines designed to burn biomass operate differently from common waste incinerators.

All this means that investors concerned with the environment should avoid any companies that are involved in the incineration of waste. The practice is wasteful, polluting, and uneconomic for communities.

COMPANIES

Thermo Tech Technologies Inc.(Langley, Canada) (TTRI.F, NASDAQ) 604-534-9346

Thermo Tech is the company with the technology mentioned at the beginning of the chapter: organic waste in one end—animal feed and fertilizer out the other. This is twenty-first century technology at its best. There are several companies with similar processes, but Thermo Tech looks like the best.

For example, the whole process of treating sewage sludge takes only 24 to 36 hours, the heat kills harmful microorganisms, and the end product, fertilizer, can be used on organic produce. A similar process turns food wastes into the dry ingredients for animal feed. This feed has found a ready market with bulk processors who incorporate it into feed for farm animals. A major pet food company has also expressed interest.

Thermo Tech plants are in the enviable position of being paid for accepting their raw materials. Just as landfills charge tipping fees to accept truckloads of garbage, the recycling plants charge similar fees. This means that the company is paid twice—once for accepting the waste and once for the finished products.

Thermo Tech can operate in partnership with a community or a private firm. After the recycling plant is built, the venture partner operates it and Thermo Tech collects a percentage of the revenues. Capital costs for a plant run about $3 million, and the payback time is just a few years. After five years of operation, gross revenues for an average plant can run as high as $5 million, with a net before taxes and interest of $2 million.

The company has ambitious expansion plans. As of this writing, several plants are already up and running in the U.S. and Canada, five are under construction, and a great many more are in the negotiation stage. In addition, the technology is being licensed to other companies. If things continue on their present course, I see Thermo Tech being one of the success stories of environmental investing during the next few years.

Resources

From Eco-Cities to Living Machines: Principles of Ecological Design, by Nancy Jack Todd and John Todd (North Atlantic Books, 1994).

The *living machines* designed by the authors are mini-ecosystems which deal with sewage in a natural manner. This is the kind of ecological solution we mentioned in Chapter 1—

one which mimics natural processes. The Todds answered the question, *How does nature deal with organic waste?*

In one model, raw sewage enters a greenhouse, where it is first exposed to nitrifying bacteria, then flows into raceways where algae multiply by taking up nutrients which are effluent (waste material). Freshwater shrimp then eat the algae and are in turn eaten by trout and bass contained in tanks at the end of the system. The effluent is slowly purified in the several days it takes for the matter to reach a plant-filled marsh, which acts as the final filter. Some of these plants, such as watercress, can be sold. At the end of this process, the effluent has turned into clear, pure water.

You can't invest in these marvelous machines yet, but you can admire the elegance of the process. A variety of living machines are already at work processing sewage in large and small operations throughout the country.

CHAPTER 8

REAL FOOD, REAL FARMING

To students of the environment, the world can sometimes look like a pretty gloomy place. Population is increasing faster than food production. While pesticides and chemical fertilizers have increased crop yields around the globe, they also tend to degrade the soil and present a danger to health—and their costs keep rising.

Given these trends, to many, the future can look a lot like the world portrayed in the film *Soylent Green,* which is so overpopulated that there is hardly room to move and so depleted of resources that bodies must be recycled into food. Even Charlton Heston can't save this world. And some environmentalists often despair of saving ours. We need another vision of the future and a means to get there.

First the vision, as seen by our cybervision, virtual reality, future-focus time goggles: In the year 2050, all of the food is grown without the use of chemical fertilizers, pesticides, or herbicides. There is still plenty of fertilizer used to keep the crop yields up, but it's all of the organic variety. The natural control of pests and weeds has evolved to the point where crops are no longer threatened.

While population levels are still high in many countries, hunger is no longer a problem. This is because most land formerly devoted to export crops has been converted into food production, and food has been distributed justly among the population. After the food riots of the 2020s, even the ruling classes realized that hunger was a cause not only of unrest, but of economic backwardness.

Much of agricultural production has reverted to small family and community-oriented farms. It is now realized that the economies of scale that allowed agribusiness to grow cheap food and other products in the twentieth century included numerous hidden costs to the environment and the consumer. There are still large farms and plantations but they practice the same sustainable agriculture as the small farms.

A CHEMICAL BATH

Sound good? Better than *Soylent Green?* Well, we have some work to do to realize this vision. Agriculture is a place where the old and the new clash in often confusing ways.

The old ways—"old" since 1945, anyway—involve dousing crops with liberal doses of pesticides, herbicides (for weeds), and fungicides. This is done in the name of increasing crop yields by eliminating the pests that destroy the plants. Other chemicals, in the form of artificial fertilizers, are added to the soil.

And crop yields do go up. Particularly in developing countries, proponents argue that this chemical agriculture is necessary to prevent starvation.

The added yields, however, are not achieved without considerable costs, many of which are hidden or deferred. In fact, chemical farming is a classic example of a technological "fix" which has backfired. For example, pest control looked very simple when DDT and other miracle products were invented: You have pests? You zap them!

Unfortunately, pesticides are not very specific. Pesticides and herbicides zap just about everything, not just pests. Helpful insects also bite the dust along with earthworms, which aerate and fertilize the soil, and beneficial microbes, which destroy many plant pathogens. Further up the food chain, wildlife, which depends on the insects for food, either dies from starvation or eats bugs that are full of toxins.

The chemicals seep into the groundwater, rendering well water—and sometimes water for whole communities—unfit to drink. Most wells in the Central Valley of California, as well as in parts of Iowa, Nebraska, and other agricultural areas are unusable. Often municipal water supplies are polluted from runoff of artificial fertilizers and pesticides. This is one reason why the Science Advisory Board to the Environmental Protection Agency warns that pesticides, herbicides, and fungicides pose one of the greatest environmental threats to Americans.

Another reason is that the chemicals also tend to poison those who work with them. An estimated 300,000 farmworkers in this country suffer from pesticide-related illnesses. In developing countries the figures are often much higher because farmers know less about how to protect themselves from the dangers. In a group of farmers studied in the Philippines, one-third had four different pesticide-related disorders.

Last, but not least, consumers who eat food grown with chemicals also eat some of the chemicals for dinner. The regulations designed to protect us from

---

Children and Pesticides

Two facts:

1. Children—especially infants—eat and drink more of certain fruits and vegetables than adults. The average one-year-old, for example, drinks 21 times more apple juice than the average adult.
2. Cancer in children is increasing.

Are these two facts connected? Many researchers think so because children, with their lower body weight and immature immune systems, may be at much greater risk from toxins in food than adults.

---

ingesting "too much" of any toxin are so inexact as to be totally ineffective in most cases.

The causes of cancer are hard to prove because tumors grow slowly over time. We do know that these chemicals are carcinogenic and that many kinds of cancer are on the rise. The overall rate of cancer in this country has increased 44 percent since 1950.

Each year in the U.S., 750 million pounds of pesticides are sprayed onto fields and orchards; these represent some 20,000 different chemical compounds. Just one percent of that quantity actually finds its way to the crops; the rest winds up in the air, water, and soil. In the midwest farm states, the soil is so saturated with chemicals that they evaporate out of the ground with water and pollute the clouds. The rain then distributes them evenly over large areas.

Ruined soil, severely damaged ecosystems, polluted drinking water, sick farmworkers, and cancer-causing chemicals in our food—these are the costs we bear so that we can buy cheap agricultural produce and support the giant corporate farms and food companies that produce the bulk of our food. But, somehow, produce doesn't seem so cheap when these hidden costs are included. The costs of growing food with chemicals are passed on to us—and to our children.

GROWIN' WHAT COMES NATURALLY

But can we get good yields from our farms and orchards without chemicals? We may have to. Five hundred species of insects and mites are now resistant to many pesticides. A number of weeds are starting to ignore herbicides, and at least 150 microbial pathogens are showing resistance to fungicides. This means that farmers are having to use more chemicals with less results. They're already paying $5 billion a year for these killers in this country and $13 billion around the world.

The costs, both the upfront and the hidden ones, have convinced many farmers to call an end to this chemical warfare aginst nature. The number of farms growing

---

Sign in Whole Foods Natural Market

"We sell only free-range, grain fed, natural meats and poultry, without added growth hormones or antibiotics, nitrates, nitrites, sulfites, or artificial preservatives, colors or flavors."

Now you know what is in meat and poultry which is *not* raised in a natural manner.

with organic methods in the U.S. now amounts to one percent of the total—and that number is increasing.

And, yes, the yields are excellent. Through a combination of clever farming methods and encouragement of natural pest predators, organic farmers have eliminated the use of chemicals, both the killers and the fertilizers. On these new farms, soil depleted by chemical farming is being enriched with organic fertilizers; worms and beneficial microbes are returning, and the entire ecosystem is repairing itself.

The United Nations Food and Agriculture Organization has trained hundreds of thousands of farmers in eight Asian countries in the use of nonchemical pest management systems (called integrated pest management or IPM). Indonesia recently banned 57 of 66 pesticides and adopted an IPM program. The rice harvest increased by 15 percent and the government saved $120 million in pesticide subsidies.

Nowadays, just about every food and beverage you can think of is grown organically or made from organically grown produce. You can even buy organic wine from a major California winery—Fetzer Vineyards—and from other wineries that buy only naturally-grown grapes.

In addition, there are many nonfood crops, such as organically grown cotton, that are finding their way into "green" manufactured goods. We will discuss more naturally grown nonfood crops in chapter 12.

THE ORGANIC REVOLUTION

There is much to be hopeful about in the new agriculture, but organically grown crops still make up only a tiny percentage of the total. We continue to drown in chemicals; these substances and other poor farming practices are ruining the soil all over the world. The United Nations

"That Called 'Cooperation!' "
—Cookie Monster

To build our new society, many of the new technologies discussed in this book will have to work together. For example, many agricultural experts are loathe to give up chemical fertilizers because they can dramatically increase crop yields. They point to crop yields doubling and tripling in developing countries where producing more food is absolutely necessary.

Organic fertilizers could take the place of the chemicals, but the supply is limited. However, as the recycling of organic wastes (described in the previous chapter) becomes commonplace, the quantity of organic fertilizer will rise dramatically.

The shift to organic, sustainable agriculture will benefit greatly from the increased amount of this organic fertilizer. And the communities that establish the composting-type recycling plants will also benefit from this shift since they will have a market for their end product.

As the new methods replace the old, we will see different sectors of the sustainable economy contribute to each other in a similar manner.

Environment Program estimates that 108 million acres of productive farmland is lost every year.

Farming with natural methods can reclaim much of this lost land. These methods conserve water and enrich the soil in addition to slowly getting rid of the chemicals.

What can we do to hasten the organic revolution? First of all, we can buy organic. There are natural food stores, both large and small, in all cities and in many smaller communities. Voting with our dollars will

> Up-to-the-minute developments include a giant vacuum device pulled and powered by a tractor. Instead of being killed by pesticides, insect pests are simply vacuumed right off the crops. And in parts of Florida, roadside weeds are being eliminated by superheated hot water instead of by herbicides.

increase the amount of food grown with natural methods—and it may eventually convince the supermarkets and food companies that they, too, had better get on the bandwagon.

Using your investment capital is another way of voting with dollars. The number of companies that produce and market organic food is still a bit thin, but there will almost certainly be more soon. Two excellent investment opportunities are described below.

COMPANIES

EarthTrade

EarthTrade is becoming an archetypal environmental company by successfully combining lofty ideals with sound business practices. Up to now, interested parties could only cheer from the sidelines; in 1995, however, the company made its first stock offering.

EarthTrade is in the business of marketing organic produce. For many years, international development organizations have promoted sustainable agriculture by providing technical and financial aid to small farmers in Latin America. EarthTrade adds a strong marketing component to these efforts. In conjunction with local nongovernmental organizations, the company provides farmers with training in organic agriculture, credit, processing of crops, shipping, and marketing.

EarthTrade currently works with cooperatives and small farmers in El Salvador, Mexico, Guatemala, Nicaragua, and North America. Organic products are marketed locally and abroad in Europe, the U.S., and Asia.

Founded in 1992, EarthTrade's balance sheet is already projected to turn positive in early 1996. The company is growing at breakneck speed. Prospective investors need to contact Progessive Asset Management (PAM) in Oakland, California, for information on the stock. While there are plans to list the stock on an exchange, this may not happen for a while. In the meantime, PAM can keep you updated on how the stock is being traded.

PAM, an investment firm specializing in socially responsible investments, is an excellent resource for social and environmental investors. PAM handles the initial offerings of many new firms of interest to the SRI community. You can learn more about PAM and get on their mailing list by calling 800-786-2998, or their New York office at 800-659-8189.

Whole Foods Markets, Inc.
(*WFMI, NASDAQ*) *512-477-4455*

Whole Foods is aiming to be the primary market chain for natural foods. Starting with one store in Austin, Texas, in 1978, Whole Foods had expanded to ten markets by 1990. In 1992, the company raised more than $22 million with a stock offering and went on a buying spree, acquiring or merging with several smaller natural foods chains. There are presently over forty stores, and Whole Foods wants to have a hundred by the year 2000.

Whole Foods markets are impressive; you may not be aware of just how many different kinds of natural foods and related products there are until you enter one. Whole Foods aids organic farmers by providing an attractive place for consumers to buy their produce.

Like most small companies, Whole Foods stock has had its ups and downs. Investors should be prepared to hold on to the stock while the company expands. As the popularity of natural foods continues to grow rapidly in the U.S., so will the fortunes of Whole Foods Market.

Wild Oats Markets

Wild Oats is the major natural foods competitor to Whole Foods. They too are growing apace, with 21 outlets in six western states, and seven more projected for 1996. Wild Oats is not presently a publicly traded company, but investors should watch carefully for an initial public offering. This is another firm that is encouraging the growth of the natural foods movement and stands to benefit greatly from this growth.

CHAPTER 9

A TRANSPORT OF DELIGHT

DARK TALES FROM THE TWENTIETH CENTURY

In the year 2050, grandparents astonish children with
stories about the olden days of darkened skies and
air that was hard to breathe. Traffic jams, constant
noise, and other horrors are carefully explained to dis-
believing young faces.

Indeed a visitor from the twentieth century would
find urban areas transformed. There are still vehicles
plying the streets and highways, but very few compared
to our time. There are many bicycles and pedestrians,
as well as some buses and trains, but the quantity of
people going from place to place seems to be drastically
reduced. Furthermore, the vehicles that are there
emit no exhaust and very little noise. The air in the
cities is as clean and fragrant as that of the surrounding
countrysides.

The origins of this reduced level of transportation
can be traced to the end of the twentieth century. By

2050, computer networks have allowed the majority of people to work from their homes or from neighborhood offices. New communities have been designed—and cities have been modified—to minimize distances from homes to necessary services. In addition, new, nonpolluting vehicles were just beginning to be introduced in the 1990s.

In this chapter, we're going to describe some of these vehicles and explain both the advantages and the disadvantages associated with them. Some of these cars are already on the streets, while others are still on the drawing boards.

First, however, we need to look at the way things are right now. This picture of present-day transportation should make the need for new kinds of vehicles crystal clear.

More Dark Tales

Returning to the noise, pollution, and inefficiencies of the twentieth century, we find that many of these problems are caused by a transportation system that runs almost entirely on oil. Transportation accounts for 63 percent of all the petroleum used in the U.S.

Eighty percent of the world's environmental pollution comes from fossil fuels. Much of this comes from industrial processes and electricity generation, but the greatest culprit is the internal combustion engine in hundreds of millions of automobiles. Serious health problems are caused by air pollution. In many cities, especially in developing countries, pollution from autos is so thick that emergency smog alert days are becoming commonplace.

Many countries must import much or all of the oil they use. In the United States, this dependence is one of the main reasons for our continuing negative trade balances.

Oil also makes for political difficulties. Since most of the oil we import comes from the volatile Middle East, we must spend a good deal of time and energy making sure our lifeline is secure. This includes spending billions on military preparedness in case we have to fight another war like the Gulf War of 1991.

The internal combustion engine is a major problem all by itself. Its efficiency in using the energy in gasoline is only about 20 percent to 25 percent. When other inefficiencies inherent in running an automobile are added in, we end up with a dismal 10 percent to 15 percent of the energy in gasoline that is actually used.

So, let's look at this picture: we spend large amounts of time and money finding oil and then even more drilling wells to bring it to the surface. It is then transported, often thousands of miles at great expense, to refineries where it's processed into gasoline and other products (more expense). Next, the gasoline is trucked to individual gas stations where we can fill the tanks in our cars. And after all this, the cars can only eke out about 15 percent of the energy in the gasoline! The rest becomes waste heat and combustion by-products that pollute the air.

Oh, and one more thing. After basing our entire transportation system and much of our economy on vehicles that burn petroleum-based products, the oil is going to run out before the year 2050. By 2037, at the present rate of consumption, all known oil reserves will be exhausted. If we add a few years for as-yet-undiscovered sources, that still only leaves us about 50 years.

This doesn't look so good. If someone came around with a business proposal that sounded like this, he would probably be shown the door pretty quickly. We have grown accustomed to these wild inefficiencies and dangers to our health only because they've been around for so long. And, of course, for a long time, they were the only game in town—or appeared to be. These days there are alternatives.

THE ELECTRIC ALTERNATIVE

In the year 1900, 38 percent of all automobiles sold were electric, 40 percent were steam, and only 22 percent were powered by internal combustion engines. This picture changed rapidly in favor of the internal combustion cars because of their range and power. Electrics hung on for a couple of decades; their cleanliness and ease of operation made them a favorite, especially of ladies. They were phased out as the gasoline cars improved their performance and became easier to drive.

Nowadays, you can buy an electric car that performs pretty much the same as your Ford or Honda. It accelerates smoothly and rapidly to highway speeds and has all the comfort and conveniences you are accustomed to. Maintenance is cheap and easy, and you will never have to go to a gas station again.

But . . . you will not be able to go too far; after 40 to 70 miles, you will need to recharge the batteries. And you will pay more for this car because it's still a specialty item; economies of scale have not yet brought the price down.

These are the disadvantages. You can't do much about the cost yet unless you are skilled enough to convert a gas vehicle to electric by yourself. But as for the range, consider how far you usually travel in your car. Statistically speaking, 80 percent of all car trips are under 20 miles. Most electrics will go at least twice that distance at freeway speeds. For families with two or more cars, therefore, including an electric as one of them could make sense.

For some advantages, let's listen to an owner of an electric, Michael Hackleman, who is also the author of *The New Electric Cars* (Chelsea Green Publishing). Here is what Michael "misses" about his gas-powered car: "I miss the oil and grunge in the 'motor' compartment. Or on my clothes and hands after I work around an engine. I miss the oil spots on the driveway. I miss periodically replacing oil filters, air filters, fan belts, plugs, points, and plug wires. Or checking, adding, or changing the oil. Or adding coolant. . . . I miss the tangle of pollution equipment. I miss smog checks. I miss waiting in gas lines. I miss pumping gas."

You might gather from the above just how much easier and cheaper electrics are to run and maintain than gasoline cars. At night—or anytime—they can be recharged simply by plugging them into an electrical outlet. Up to now, the reduced maintenance costs have been balanced by the need to replace the battery pack every two to three years. This drawback is being remedied, as we will see.

On a large scale, the mass use of electric vehicles (EVs) would greatly reduce the evils of the oil economy just listed. EVs are much more efficient users of energy than internal combustion engines. And the utility energy they use is likely to come from other sources than oil (oil fires only about five percent of utility generators in the U.S.).

Although the EVs themselves produce no pollution, the utility turbines, of course, do. Smokestack pollution, however, is controlled much more easily than the exhaust of millions of cars. Even factoring in the increased production of electricity, the use of EVs on a mass scale would dramatically reduce most forms of pollution.

Furthermore, EVs can be charged by any electric source, including solar or wind. Some EV owners charge their batteries with solar panels. A few electrics have photovoltaic cells built into their roofs and hoods. This area is not nearly enough to power the car while it's running, but the cells can contribute significantly to charging the batteries when the car is driven or parked in the sun.

BETTER BATTERIES—FINALLY!

There are other advances that are making the electric auto sound like a winner these days. For a long time, primitive battery technology was cited as the main reason for the delay in EV production. For example, the number of lead-acid batteries required to power an automobile adds considerable weight to the vehicle, they take a long time to recharge, they can only drive a car 40 to 80 miles, and they need to be replaced every two to three years. (These lead-acid batteries are roughly similar to the common type found in most passenger vehicles today.)

R & D to the rescue! Battery research is finally bearing some fruit. There are several new types being researched; some are actually in operation. Of these, the most promising are the nickel-metal-hydride types and the zinc-air.

The nickel-metal-hydride type of battery, while promising, is still in the research stage; 1998 is the projected year the technology will be ready. The zinc-air battery, however, is already being used in extensive field trials.

The Electric Fuel Corporation, an Israel-based company, is well along in the development of a workable zinc-air battery system. The system, which is presently undergoing trials with the German Postal Service (Deutsche Bundespost), is rated at 200 watt hours per kilogram, as opposed to 40 watt hours per kilogram for a lead-acid battery. A Mercedes van that traveled 47 miles with a lead-acid battery pack went 200 miles with a zinc-air pack.

Instead of recharging, a spent battery pack is removed from the vehicle and replaced with a renewed pack in a matter of minutes. The spent batteries are then sent to a regeneration facility. This operation, of course, requires the kind of centralized facility for a fleet of vehicles that a large organization like the Bundespost has. A consumer operation of this sort would require an extensive support system of service stations and regeneration centers.

In terms of cost, when mass produced, the zinc-air systems will be roughly $100 per kilowatt/hour of energy storage capacity, or about the same as a lead-acid system. Electric Fuel anticipates that the cost of the battery system will be roughly equal to that of an internal combustion engine, drive train, and fuel tank. As economies of scale come into play, operating costs could come down to as little as five cents a mile.

In the U.S., where gasoline prices hover around $1.20 to $1.40 per gallon, operating costs for an internal combustion vehicle are between four and five cents a mile. In Europe, however, where gas is highly taxed, operating costs are closer to ten or eleven cents a mile. This is why Electric Fuel is concentrating its efforts on Europe instead of America.

Another company, the Zinc Air Power Corporation has taken a different tack with zinc-air batteries. Its battery modules can be recharged in the vehicle and will drive an average car 250 miles at an average speed of 45 mph.

Wait a minute, did we say *250 miles?* What happened to the 40 to 80 mile range we mentioned before? Well, that shorter range was accomplished using lead-acid batteries, which are still used in most EVs. The zinc-air modules are much more efficient. As you can see, the new research is moving very fast.

The engineers at Zinc Air are still working with these batteries, specifically at increasing the number of recharge cycles. They're now up to 190 cycles and their eventual goal is 400 cycles. Watch for these batteries to hit the streets in just a few years. And something else to watch for: in two to three years Zinc Air plans to go public.

. . . AND BETTER BATTERY CHARGERS

Even the venerable lead-acid battery is looking better these days. Recently, a new charging technology has appeared that not only charges the batteries much faster, but greatly extends their usable life.

In 1991, Electronic Power Technology, Inc. (EPTI), started out by simply trying to extend the life of batteries of all kinds—batteries in flashlights, radios, computers, and so on. They succeeded in this; their charging systems are now used not just to recharge, but to rejuvenate failed batteries used in small electronic devices.

In 1993, however, they realized they had a market in the arena of larger batteries, specifically, those used in electric vehicles. The EPTI technology has several dramatic advantages over traditional charging systems for EVs:

1. Batteries can be charged in as little as 18 minutes, versus 4 to 8 hours for conventional chargers.

2. Charging efficiencies are over 95 percent versus about 65 percent for other methods. This means less electricity used.

3. Batteries can be charged to 100 percent of capacity, versus about 80 percent for other systems. This extends the range of EVs.

4. Battery life is extended by a factor of two to four times. This means that EV owners will rarely have to replace their battery pack.

5. The EPTI recharging method works on other types of batteries besides lead-acid: nickel-metal-hydride, nickel-cadmium, and zinc-air, for example.

With these new types of batteries and charging systems, the prospects have changed for electric vehicles. This is the kind of technology that will make EVs a viable form of transportation.

How about viable investments in such technology? Well, EPTI has tentative plans to go public in 1996. Watch for this IPO (initial public offering) very carefully. A company with this kind of revolutionary technology could do extremely well.

OTHER STORAGE SYSTEMS

Better batteries are not the only energy storage systems in the works. In computers and small electronic appliances, there are devices called capacitors. Capacitors store electricity by allowing a charge to build up between two conductive plates separated by an insulator. They operate very efficiently, but up until recently have been used for only very small charges.

In the research labs, capacitors are being scaled up and improved. New, advanced prototypes—called ultracapacitors—may be ready for testing in 1996 and might be used in EVs sometime in the next few years. The ultracapacitors could be several times cheaper than comparable battery systems and would last much longer.

You may have noticed that there are a lot of "might be's" and "may be's" when speaking of innovative storage systems. This is also true of the flywheel. Advanced flywheel energy-storage systems have been worked on since the 1970s; periodically, some research firm announces an exciting new development and receives a lot of press. Then flywheels retreat into oblivion until the next new development.

Flywheels store energy by spinning at speeds of more than 100,000 revolutions per minute. Until new composite materials were fabricated, speeds like this were impossible; the flywheel rotor would simply disintegrate. Now, however, the flywheels can be spun up to top speeds by a power source and then made to turn a generator on demand.

The light weight of composite flywheels have made them attractive candidates to replace batteries or to provide extra power on demand to battery-driven cars. Like capacitors, commercial use of flywheels seems to be a few years down the road, but this is a very exciting technology, one to keep a close eye on.

Industry and government are finally devoting real money to making EVs happen. There is so much happening that we have been able to touch on just the high points of that research here. But now, let's take a look at what a truly innovative vehicle might look like. This is the kind of inclusive design that will eventually revolutionize our transportation system.

A TRANSPORT OF DELIGHT

In the 1970s, this writer went around asking those in the know why it wouldn't make sense to place a small gasoline (or other fuel) engine in an electric car. This engine would run at a constant speed, which would greatly increase efficiency while cutting pollution. The engine would power the car through a generator and charge the batteries, but it would only be started for longer trips; the car would be plugged in at night and this recharging would take care of most around-town driving.

I even wrote an article on this concept in 1974. It seemed to me then—and it still seems—that this hybrid vehicle would solve the main problem with electrics, that of limited range of driving, while adding very little pollution to the air. This would be the missing link that would finally make EVs feasible.

I got different answers from the engineers I talked to. "It's been tried" was the most common. "The engine, generator, and fuel tank would add too much weight" was another. "Too inefficient—the engine needs to drive the car directly." "Too polluting—electrics have to be totally clean." "Too complex—too much hardware." "Too expensive." And so on.

Although I was never really satisfied with these answers, there wasn't much I could do. While knowledgeable about renewable technology, I'm not a scientist or engineer. I was going mostly on intuition and what I felt was common sense.

In fact, engineers have been working on this and other forms of hybrid vehicles for quite a while. Until recently, however, the experimental models most in favor used "parallel" drive systems: the fueled engine would drive the car directly at certain times, then switch off and the electric motor would take over. The "series" approach, as described, in which the engine would power the electric motor through a generator, seemed to be out of favor.

Now, however, this kind of vehicle is finally coming into its own; several companies and research organizations are devoting time and money to the series hybrid-electric auto. In particular, Amory Lovins and the folks at Rocky Mountain Institute (see *Resources*) have worked out an elegant design for what they call a "supercar." This design is elegant because it solves so many problems at once. Because every facet of the vehicle is designed from scratch, the synergy results in a vehicle that performs several levels above the vehicles of today.

EV technology has been held back by attempts to fit it into old forms—those of vehicles designed for internal combustion engines. The majority of EVs on the road today, in fact, are just production cars with their insides taken out and replaced with electric components. But real technological change usually involves starting from somewhere else, which is what the supercar does.

So what puts the "super" in supercar? First of all, it is superlight. Built of molded polymer composites such as carbon-fiber, an early model might weigh as little as 1,275 pounds, or roughly one-half the weight of a comparable four passenger auto today. Second, the supercar is aerodynamically designed to drastically reduce drag from air resistance.

The braking system is designed to recover the energy used to stop the car; when braking, the electric motor is temporarily turned into a generator, which slows the car and recharges the batteries. Especially in city driving, this regenerative braking can increase fuel efficiency by 25 percent.

The supercar is driven by a battery pack that, in advanced models, would power the cars' electric motors for most short trips. But this pack is small and, therefore, much lighter than the massive battery modules found in most electrics. The pack is recharged by plugging it into an electric outlet or, perhaps, from photovoltaic cells on the roof of the car.

A fueled engine kicks in for longer trips, powering a generator that runs the electric motor and charges the battery pack. Because this engine runs at a constant speed, it can be sized for average demand instead of peak demand. The extra power needed for peak demand—fast acceleration and hill climbing—comes from the batteries. Average demand leaves us with a small engine continually running at its most efficient speed, and this translates into very high fuel economy.

Early models of the supercar would probably employ a small, gasoline-driven internal combustion engine, but later models might run on fuel cells or engines powered by less polluting fuels such as hydrogen (more about hydrogen and fuel cells later).

So what kind of fuel economy are we talking about here? What's fascinating about designing such a car from the ground up is that while each design change may only contribute only a small amount to fuel savings, they often reinforce each other. This synergy ultimately results in dramatic increases in fuel efficiency. The supercar should achieve about 150 miles to a gallon of gas, with a load of four adults, in normal driving conditions. Later models with more exotic engines or fuel cells would do even better.

Passengers cars and other light-duty vehicles use about 60 percent of the oil in the U.S. But the supercar technology also lends itself to upsizing, which means that many large vehicles could become part of this fuel efficiency revolution.

Such savings would not only positively impact our economy by cutting the amount of oil we need, but would eliminate a large percentage of transportation-related pollution. And this would be accomplished by cars and trucks with much the same power, range, and conveniences we are accustomed to in our present vehicles.

There is more to the supercar than we can include here. See *Resources* for information on how to order a complete paper on the supercar from the Rocky Mountain Institute. The paper includes a fascinating description of possible changes in the American economy which might occur as a result of the shift to manufacturing this kind of vehicle (for one, because the supercar is built mostly from composites, the market for steel would drastically decrease).

We have been describing the supercar in the present tense here, but we are speaking of the design, not the actual vehicle. A few experimental cars have been built that incorporate some features of this design, most notably Paul MacReady's Sunraycer, which has competed in several electric car races, and the General Motors Ultralite.

But while such vehicles may still be mostly on the drawing board, the advantages of this technology are so compelling that we can soon expect to see great changes in the automotive world. Investors should carefully watch developments in this field over the next five to ten years; it may well be that the large automakers will not be the only players. And in any case, small suppliers of the necessary components will grow as the industry grows.

This is a case where the Big Three car manufacturers will be forced to start making big changes or be left behind by more progressive automakers in this country or other countries. The supercars are coming; the main question is who is going to be the first to develop them.

1998

In an attempt to encourage the manufacture of zero emission vehicles (ZEVs), several major states have mandated that by 1998, 2 percent of cars sold in these states must be ZEVs. Because more exotic, nonpolluting technologies are not yet practical, right now, this means electric cars.

Whether these mandates will actually take effect is questionable. The automakers are arguing that they're not ready, and the small companies don't have enough capacity to fill the need. It may be that the dates will be pushed back to allow more time for compliance.

While environmentalists can only applaud the spirit of such mandates, these mandates have the unfortunate effect of concentrating only on *zero* emission technology. This eliminates extremely low emission vehicles, such as the hybrid supercars. Pure electric cars do cause pollution, of course, even though the amount is greatly reduced by placing the power source at the electric generating plant. But the vehicles themselves put out no toxic gases, and this fulfills the requirements of the mandates.

But, in fact, advanced hybrids would probably produce less overall pollution than pure electric cars. This is largely because the battery systems weigh so much in pure electrics. In the supercar, the small engine, generator, and fuel tank weigh substantially less than the 650 to 900 pounds of lead-acid batteries in most electric cars. The amount of fuel used is less because the weight is less.

Three things need to happen here to speed up the development of low-emission vehicles. First, the state regulatory bodies have to take a second look at their mandates. The requirements need to be altered to include very low emission vehicles whose *overall* emissions are equal to those of electric vehicles.

Second, the states need to initiate more discussions with the automakers on how to bring these new vehicles to the marketplace. The car companies do have real concerns that need to be addressed. Designing, manufacturing, and marketing radically new vehicles is a risky, cost-intensive business. Service centers need to be set up, and repair personnel trained, among other things.

But, in spite of these difficulties, the third thing that needs to happen is that Detroit needs to work harder to make electric or hybrid vehicles a reality in this country.

It *is* possible to produce electrics on a large scale. In France, Peugeot-Citroen is now producing a subcompact electric and soon expects to be selling 10,000 of these a year. American automakers should be encouraged (and, perhaps, concerned) by the number of EVs beginning to appear on European streets.

FUEL CELLS

If petroleum burned in internal combustion engines makes for a transportation system from hell ("infernal" combustion), then fuel cells must have been inspired by the other place. The most advanced fuel cells efficiently burn hydrogen and oxygen and produce as their only waste product—(fanfare)—pure *water!* ([H]ydrogen + [O]xygen = H_2O, which is water.)

Fuel cells are devices that transform hydrogen and oxygen into electricity. They are roughly similar to batteries in that they have positive and negative terminals, electrodes, and an electrolyte, and they produce a flow of electric power. Unlike batteries, however, fuel cells do not store energy, but produce electricity from continuously supplied fuel.

This fuel—hydrogen—can be produced by a variety of different sources, including natural gas, methanol, oil, coal, and electrolyzed water (passing an electric current through water divides it into hydrogen and oxygen). Because hydrogen is present in all these fuels, it can be separated out by chemical processes. Stripping hydrogen from natural gas is the cheapest method now available.

Natural gas or gasoline can be carried on a vehicle and hydrogen produced on board. Some of the experimental vehicles now in operation use this method. Others, such as the "Genesis Zero Emission Transporter," produced by Energy Partners in Florida, store hydrogen in an onboard fuel tank.

Experimental is the operative word here. While fuel cells have been around for quite a while (first invented in 1839), intensive research has been going on only since 1990. This is already bearing fruit, but a commercial fuel cell competitive with present power sources is still a ways off. Specifically, the power-to-weight ratio must be increased for use in vehicles, reliability in all weather conditions improved, and absolutely safe storage of the volatile hydrogen must be achieved, in addition to a raft of other technical problems. When these are solved, production costs should eventually be comparable to present systems, perhaps less, as the technology improves.

The rewards of this research, however, will be tremendous. There are powerful reasons why most people in the field of renewable energy are excited by fuel cells.

First, there is efficiency: by converting chemical energy directly to electricity, fuel cells achieve efficiencies two to three times higher than internal combustion engines. Next, there is cleanliness: most experimental vehicles with fuel cells are zero emission vehicles.

Long life and low maintenance of the cells will make running costs less than present cars and trucks. And, finally, fuel cells run quietly; cities with vehicles run by fuel cells will be more pleasant places without the constant noise pollution of the internal combustion engine.

Fuel cell vehicles combine the best properties of the electric car with the long range and quick fueling of present-day vehicles. An advanced design of the supercar uses a fuel cell instead of a gas engine to power its generator; this pushes its possible fuel rating up to 250 to 300 miles per gallon.

There are quite a few other uses just waiting for fuel cell technology to be improved. For example, navies in different countries have announced plans to use fuel cells as propulsion systems for ships, particularly submarines, because they produce no toxic exhaust.

The cells can also be used for stationary power production on a small or large scale. This will allow utilities to expand their systems without building large, costly, polluting power plants.

And, as we will see in the next section, fuel cells can be part of the energy system for the solar economy we talked about in chapter 4.

HYDROGEN

Hydrogen and fuel cells go together. They will be two of the most important links in the power system of the twenty-first century. But hydrogen has other uses, too. It is a gas that can cook your food, just like natural gas or propane; it can be a storage system for renewable energy sources; and it can be used as a fuel in many applications, including jet aircraft.

So when renewable energy experts speak of the future "hydrogen-based economy," they are referring to an economy that uses this clean-burning fuel for almost every power application.

We have here another instance of two new technologies working together synergistically. As the costs of producing electricity from renewable sources go down, hydrogen can be economically made by electrolysis. For example, a photovoltaic panel might provide the electricity to run a current through a tank of water. This process produces pure hydrogen, which would be stored for future use.

Electrolysis of this sort is the cleanest way to produce hydrogen because it involves no fossil fuels. Another advantage is that it can be done on a small scale, such as in your home. Here's how the hydrogen-based economy would look in the microcosm of your home:

When the sun is out, the photovoltaic panels on your roof, besides providing power to the house, would also produce hydrogen, which would be stored in a tank in the basement or shed. Then, at night or on cloudy days, the hydrogen would power a generator or fuel cell to provide your household electricity.

In addition, you could also fill the fuel tank in your car with this hydrogen. For short trips, the car battery pack would be charged by the house PV system, but for longer trips, the fuel cell in the vehicle would take over. *And* the hydrogen from the tank in the basement would be piped to your furnace, water heater, and cooking stove!

This is what is meant by a complete hydrogen-based economy. The hydrogen is essentially made from sunlight and water and when it burns, the waste product is water. With technology like this, we're getting closer to highly efficient natural systems such as plant photosynthesis.

The process of making hydrogen by electrolysis using renewable energy sources can be jacked up to a scale useful to the utilities. In 2050, the giant PV arrays and wind generators make great quantities of the gas; then, at night or on cloudy, windless days, the hydrogen runs the generating system.

A word about safety: Hydrogen is volatile both in gas and liquid form, but working with it will require no more care than working with gasoline or natural gas. Or, in other words, dealing safely with hydrogen requires special attention, but no more so than we are used to. Safe and effective storage is one of the problems engineers are currently working on.

The clean skies in the year 2050, as well as the thriving world economy, are in no small part dependent on the use of nature's most plentiful element. In addition, because burning hydrogen produces no carbon dioxide, the fear of global warming from burning fossil fuels will be no more than a bad memory.

TRAINS, PLANES, AND . . . RAIL CARS?

We have dealt primarily with the automobile in this chapter because this is where most of the opportunities for individual investors will come from. The transportation system of the future, however, will also include great innovations in public transportation. Large vehicles, such as buses, will be driven by nonpolluting fuel cells. Ships, too, will employ this efficient power source.

Magnetic-levitation trains, riding a few inches above the tracks, will carry passengers smoothly and quietly at speeds up to 300 miles per hour. This kind of speed will enable trains to replace increasingly crowded airplanes on short intercity runs.

While advanced personal vehicles may solve problems such as pollution and overdependence on oil, other problems related to road traffic such as congestion, accidents, and long commute times will remain. These must be solved by better urban design, changes in the workplace (such as working at home over the computer networks), and improved public transport systems. Or, perhaps, these improvements might be augmented by an entirely new transportation system, designed from scratch . . .

My favorite candidate for a new transportation system is the personal rail car. The rail car will combine the privacy and convenience of automobiles with the ease and safety of public transportation. A monorail network as extensive as our present system of roads and highways will replace the old system, along with most road vehicles.

Individuals and families will own rail cars instead of autos; the cars will be about the same size, but instead of driving them, you will simply punch in your destination and then sit back and look at the scenery. So as not to interfere with pedestrians and bicycles, the tracks are elevated, and this allows for much higher speeds than road-bound traffic. In fact, the rail cars travel fast enough to replace trains and airplanes in intercity travel of a few hundred miles.

Rail cars are being developed in a few places, but investors should not hold their breath waiting for companies with this technology. This is, at present, no more than an interesting futuristic concept, and I present it here simply to fill out our picture of innovative transportation.

COMPANIES

While there are only a few public companies presently involved in innovative vehicle systems, investors will not have to wait long. Research is proceeding rapidly all over the world. Many of the small companies doing this R & D will probably go public; many others will start up. This is a field ready to explode, and a large section of it will be occupied by small cap firms.

In particular, we should expect to see a number of small companies involved in electric vehicle production and related activities. Right now, there is only one publicly held electric vehicle firm and they are experiencing great financial difficulties. U.S. Electricar expanded too fast for a still-limited market and had to declare chapter 11 bankruptcy in 1995.

The company will probably emerge from chapter 11 soon, but investors should wait until the firm looks stable again. As the market for alternative vehicles grows, U.S. Electricar may yet be a player. In the meantime, keep your eyes out for other firms in the field going public.

Electric Fuel Corporation (*EFCX, NASDAQ*) *212-230-2172*

This Israel-based company is traded on NASDAQ. The stock has done well recently as a result of the firm's success in negotiating further contracts in Germany and Sweden. If the tests being run by the German Postal Service pan out—and, so far, they look very promising—other government and private fleets could start using the technology. Electric Fuel looks very good, as of this writing.

* * *

Watch closely for initial public offerings by Electronic Power Technology, Inc., and the Zinc Air Power Corporation. Efficient batteries are hot news because electric vehicles need them to become competitive with gasoline vehicles.

Resources

Rocky Mountain Institute. 1739 Snowmass Creek Road, Old Snowmass, CO 81654-9199. 303-927-3851. FAX: 303-927-4178.
Some of the most innovative environmental thinking comes from this place high in the Rocky Mountains. Environmentalists can keep up-to-date and investors can learn what the technology of tomorrow is likely to look like. For information on joining the Institute or a catalog of their many publications, call.

CHAPTER 10

MARKETING THE TWENTY-FIRST CENTURY

MOVING TOWARD 2050

By 2050, the distinction between environmentally friendly products and other products will have ended. *All* goods and services will be part of the sustainable economy, whether they are recycled or simply manufactured in a responsible manner.

Exciting things are happening on the way to creating this kind of economy. In 1989, the Netherlands enacted its National Environmental Policy Plan (NEPP) with the ambitious goal of creating a sustainable economy in one generation.

The plan starts with the government setting national environmental goals, with the help of consultants from each industry. Consumers and industry can reach these goals by whatever methods they choose.

127

Government incentives and support provide assistance, but if the goals are not reached by the target date, regulations and penalties go into effect. This is the classic carrot-and-stick approach.

As an example, in 1990, representatives from the Dutch construction industry met with officials of the NEPP and developed a working plan to reach the environmental targets. This plan included such goals as using tropical hardwood only from sustainably managed forests and increasing the use of nontropical wood by 20 percent, both by 1995; increasing the use of demolition and construction waste from 60 percent in 1990 to 90 percent by 2000; and increasing the use of low-solvent paint to at least 50 percent by 1995.

Since the construction plan went into effect, there has been a substantial drop in toxic pollutants produced by the industry. In addition, sustainable building regulations have gone into effect. Similar plans are now operating in every sector of the Dutch economy.

While applauding this plan, many people doubt that such far-reaching programs could ever find a place in our corporate-dominated American economy. But, lo and behold, here is a state delegation from New Jersey visiting the Netherlands in 1994 to learn about the NEPP. Now, New Jersey is considering adapting the Dutch plan to the needs of their state economy. The first step, according to State Chief of Policy and Planning, Jane Kenny, will be to "hold round-table dialogues with industry leaders, with environmentalists, with farmers, with health professionals, and with . . . citizens."

The Resource Renewal Institute is currently bringing the Dutch model to the attention of state governments all over the country. Their hope is that if it catches on, the federal government will eventually adopt such a plan.

We, as citizens, consumers, and investors can do a great deal to bring about a sustainable economy. As

A Better Way?

We live in an adversarial society. In chapter 1, we
described how auto manufacturers often react badly
to government regulations. This is the way it happens in most cases: a government agency, such as the
Environmental Protection Agency (EPA), announces
its plans for new regulations of an industry. The industry executives then announce that these rules are
impossible to fulfill and begin to hire lawyers and lob-
byists (at great expense) to kill any Congressional
bills containing the new regulations. The whole issue
becomes a great public struggle, with the industry
and its supporters on one side and the environmentalists and their supporters on the other. If a bill does
get passed, it usually pleases nobody.

Could it be that the Dutch environmental plan is
a better way of doing business? Would it be possible
to get auto executives, environmentalists, consumer
groups, and the EPA to sit around a table and discuss
the problem?

"Look," says the EPA representative, "we all know
that we've got to start moving toward electric and
hybrid vehicles. If we don't do it, the Japanese and
Europeans will. Now what's the best way of doing
this? The government can provide some assistance
and tax breaks, but we want some real planning and
some reasonable target dates."

It seems that this approach would have to work
better than the messy, expensive, and ultimately
unsatisfying method we now employ. Starting off by
concentrating on how all parties concerned can work
together for a common goal just might be a better
way than focusing on their differences.

citizens, we can support the adoption of such plans as the Dutch model. As investors, we can support those companies that are moving us into a sustainable twenty-first century. And as consumers, we need to vote with our dollars and buy the kind of products that are energy efficient and produced in an environmentally responsible manner.

Some of these kinds of products can be purchased from regular retail stores. For many of them, however, consumers have to go to outlets that sell only products that promote and sustain the environment. Right now, we're going to take a look at one of the best of these new marketing firms, one which has turned itself into an exemplary environmental company.

A REAL GOOD CENTER

In the small town of Hopland, California, about two and a half hours north of San Francisco, a new center is rising. Called the Solar Living Center, it will incorporate a retail showroom for environmental products, several educational living structures, and a beautifully landscaped garden.

This center is being built by the Real Goods Trading Company, a catalog and retail firm based in the town of Ukiah (half an hour north of Hopland). Real Goods sells renewable energy products, recycled goods, and many other products with environmental connections. Started in 1978 by now President John Schaeffer as a retail store, the company shifted its emphasis to mail order in the early 1980s. Sales have continued to grow ever since, reaching a net of over $16 million in fiscal 1995. (Real Goods' fiscal year ends in April.) Retailing has not been forgotten, however. In addition to the outlet in Hopland,

California, Real Goods has recently opened stores in Eugene, Oregon, and Amhearst, Wisconsin.

Real Goods has emerged not just as a leading marketer of environmental products, but as an educational center. The company is actually involved in three complementary activities: education about renewable technology, selling home-based renewable energy, and marketing environmentally friendly products for the home. Many firms mentioned in this book have environmental products and many of their managers and personnel are also dedicated to improving the environment. But few have the environmental ethos so completely built into the structure of the company as Real Goods.

As an example, the first few pages of the company's annual report, before any mention of balance sheets or statements of earnings, contain the yearly "Eco-Audit." Stockholders learn how much paper was recycled in the company offices (including how many trees and the amount of water and power that were saved as a result), the company's total energy use, and how much fuel was used by employees getting to work. All glass and aluminum are recycled. Food waste at the Operations Department is composted and used to nourish plants around the building. A "Green Team" is being established to coordinate these efforts.

This dedication to sustainable practices and to educating not just its customers, but whoever else will listen, makes Real Goods an archetypal environmental company—one that can serve as an example to others. This is one reason why we're devoting so much space to it in this chapter.

Another reason is that it provides a standard for investors. Other companies involved in sustainable technology may not operate according to the same guidelines as Real Goods, but you, as a stockholder can demand that they do. Call up the investor relations departments of the firms in your portfolio and ask if their company reports are printed on recycled paper. Go to a stockholders' meeting and ask the managers if they have a plan to reduce energy use in their offices, or if they operate an in-house recycling program. Ask . . . well, you get the idea.

AN ENVIRONMENTAL FAMILY

Real Goods's dedication to the environment is also what makes the company popular with its customers. Most of them are also committed to living lightly on the planet and they buy products that help them do that. They also offer suggestions, helpful information, and no small amount of criticism in the large Readers' Forum of the *Real Goods News*. This magazine on sustainable technology and product listings is published quarterly in addition to the Real Goods Catalog (also quarterly).

The 650-page *Solar Living Sourcebook* is a combination of a catalog of hundreds of ecologically friendly products, a how-to book on installing renewable energy, and a fund of information on environmental technology and related topics. Information sections of 10 to 20 pages in the latest Sourcebook have titles such as "Home and Market Gardening," "Mobility and Electric Vehicles," "Shelter," and "Livelihood and Learning."

In the appendix, a visionary article on sustainable energy by Amory Lovins is followed by thirty pages of detailed instructions on how to make your photovoltaic power system conform to the National Electrical Code. It is this combination of vision and nuts-and-bolts practicality that endears Real Goods to its customer-subscribers.

It is also these customer-subscribers who make up the bulk of the 5,000 stockholders. This is a prime example of investing in what you know about; these stockholders not only have firsthand knowledge of the Real

Goods Trading Company, but most of them are also knowledgeable about sustainable technology.

A Renewable Education

Real Goods holds weekend and weeklong workshops for those interested in getting their homes "off the grid" (meaning the utility grid). The company's Institute for Solar Living teaches practical applications of renewable technology at retreat centers in Northern California and in a few other states.

Also available for inspection to would-be off-the-gridders are 33 energy-independent homes around the country. Real Goods sells renewable energy equipment at a discount to the owners of these homes in return for opening their homes to the public on a limited basis.

When the Solar Living Center in Hopland is completed in 1996, all the renewable technology needed to run a home will be not only on display, but operating. All power for the center will come from solar and wind. Energy-efficient lighting and appliances will be up and running. Even the garden will be educational, a living demonstration of edible plants and various North American ecosysytems.

Sometime in 1997, the company plans to open a bed-and-breakfast inn as part of the center. This will be an energy-independent house where guests will have a first-hand experience of living with renewable, energy-efficient technology.

LOOKING AHEAD

The nineties have not been easy years for companies selling environmental products. Be it the recession of the early part of the decade or the anti-environmental sentiment in some circles, falling sales have caused some firms to fail, others to retrench their operations. Even Real Goods, which has boasted rising profits from year one, expects sales to level off in 1996, at least temporarily.

John Schaeffer feels that the company has been hit less hard than others because of the loyalty of its customers and their dedication to the environment. It is these kinds of consumers who will ensure the ultimate success of Real Goods and other companies like it. My feeling is that the market for environmental goods will begin to expand once more as consumers learn more about the advantages of sustainable technology.

Real Goods Trading Corporation
(RGT, PACIFIC STOCK EXCHANGE) **707-468-9292**

CHAPTER 11

CLEANING UP POLLUTION IN ADVANCE

THE FUEL THAT NEVER WAS

This chapter should appeal to science fiction buffs, because it involves dealing with a future problem before it begins. For starters, let's suppose that someone from the year 2020 traveled back in time to our decade in the late twentieth century.

"Listen," says this time traveler, "we've got big problems with pollution, waste, and shortages in 2020. So we're requesting that you cut back on your use of raw materials and use less energy. Since most of you will still be alive in 2020, you'll be doing yourselves a favor as well as your children. You'll also make us . . . I mean, you . . . whoever, much richer from the money you save."

Unlike most sci-fi stories, this one can actually become a reality. We can save tremendous amounts of

Reducing the National (Energy) Deficit

We are a profligate society. We throw money around, then complain that we have a budget deficit larger than the total economies of most countries. This is beginning to change, but a more rapid rate of change could save us a lot of money.

Energy efficiency is important stuff; it can make or break giant economies like our own. Because Japan uses energy more efficiently, they spend only 5 percent of their gross national product (GNP) on energy, as opposed to our 11.2 percent. This means that the Japanese have a 6 percent edge over us in the manufacture and sale of products in the world markets.

fuel and raw materials, eliminate millions of tons of polluting gases, and save billions of dollars by simply employing more efficient practices. We're not speaking here of cutting back, but rather of getting the same amount of convenience from drastically less energy. It's cheaper *not* to burn fuel.

In fact, we have already been doing this. From 1979 to 1986, this country got *seven times* as much new energy from savings as from all net increases in supply. The monetary savings to consumers and industry have been estimated at $150 billion a year. This is "the fuel that never was." Amory Lovins, of the Rocky Mountain Institute, calls it "negawatts" or "negabarrels" (of oil).

Lovins has calculated that "the best technologies on the market can save about three-quarters of all electricity now used in the United States, while providing unchanged or improved service." Electricity production accounts for about one-third of fossil fuel use. But similar

savings are possible in fuel to heat and cool our buildings, power our vehicles, and run our industries.

This means that instead of investing in more expensive fossil fuel plants, we would do better to invest in
these new energy-saving technologies. They're cheaper
than building new power plants, they're nonpolluting,
and they conserve natural resources.

Many utilities are beginning to realize this. In 1990,
Pacific Gas & Electric (in Northern California) saved
itself $15 million by helping its customers eliminate
280 million kWh of electricity. Southern California Edison gave away a half-million energy-efficient light bulbs
to its customers; the savings in reduced production of
electricity more than paid for the cost of the bulbs.

How do utilities make money by selling less energy?
By reducing customer demand, they avoid having to
build more generating facilities, which are extremely
expensive. So, although they may make somewhat less
income, they save so much more on the unbuilt power
plants, that they come out far ahead.

These new, energy-saving technologies will replace
the old during the coming decades not just because
they're more ecologically sound, but because they're better in every way—they save money and improve the
quality of life. Let's take a look at some efficient systems,
starting with the natural world.

A MORE EFFICIENT WORLD

The natural world is a model of efficiency. The demands
of survival have caused each species to evolve into its
most effective form. Those that could not evolve fast
enough became extinct. Nothing is wasted in this world;
everything provides food for something else; everything
is recycled.

Solar Collectors
(The Photosynthetic Kind)

A flat black coating has been the accepted norm for
solar collector panels because black absorbs the most
available light . . . or does it? In the 1970s, one solar
firm discovered that a certain shade of green actually
absorbs slightly more light than black. This green
was—you guessed it—the same color employed for
millions of years by those original solar collectors:
plants. This is yet another example of the kind of
thing we can learn from the ecology experts in the
natural world.

Life on Earth, of course, has had a billion or so years
to perfect this system. Humankind has had less than a
million—and only a few millennia of employing more
complex technology. Most of that time, of course, was
spent simply discovering better ways to survive. Only in
the last few decades have we begun to take a close look at
our effect on the planet and at cleaner, more efficient
ways of doing things.

We have operated, until recently, on the assumption
that more is better. More food, more and bigger housing,
more machines, more transportation, more people. Only
in the last few years have we begun to see that our quality of life can be adversely affected by just increasing the
quantity of everything.

Raising the efficiency of technology is one of the keys
to improving quality of life without sacrificing convenience. Up to now, our industrialized society has put
most of its energy into getting more from more. Getting
more from less involves a major shift in consciousness—
one which may save us from ourselves. This shift can

even be seen as an attempt by the human species to evolve before we eliminate ourselves by destroying our environment.

CREATING MONEY FROM NEGAWATTS

So, where are all these savings going to come from? Can we really reduce our energy bill by three-quarters?

First of all, the savings are going to come from buildings. Our homes, businesses, and public buildings have been prodigal wasters of energy, leaky as old fishing boats, pouring expensive heat or cooling back into the environment. Did your mom ever tell you to close the door because "we can't afford to heat up the whole outside?" This is what most buildings have been doing, even with the doors closed.

Apply energy-efficient techniques to existing buildings and you can cut utility bills in half. Incorporate them into the design of new buildings and the savings rise to as high as 75 percent.

Most of these techniques, especially with existing structures, are pretty low-tech. They include insulating the walls and ceiling, and weather-stripping around the doors and windows. Extra insulation around the water heater will save 25 percent of what you pay for hot water. Insulating is popular with utility companies these days; many will give you rebates for adding insulation to your home.

Raising the tech level a bit brings us to low-emissivity films (low-E films). When applied to the inside of windows, they reflect back 55 percent of the sun's heat, cutting cooling bills in summer. Then, in the winter, they cut heating bills by reflecting heat back into the house.

The energy elves have also been at work on the humble light bulb. We're familiar with fluorescent lights as long tubes in overhead fixtures; we now need to start familiarizing ourselves with their new incarnations as light bulbs. Fluorescents use about a quarter as much power as incandescent bulbs while producing the same amount of light. They also last ten times longer.

The new, high-quality bulbs have none of the glare and flicker common to fluorescents, and they fit most lamps. While the initial cost of the bulbs is still high, the energy they save, coupled with their long life, makes for substantial savings in cash. For example, a fluorescent bulb, providing light equivalent to a 75-watt incandescent bulb, will save about $30.00 over its life of 4.5 years. Add up the number of light bulbs in your house, and you can see that we're talking real money here.

In fact, such investments in efficient use of energy will get you a guaranteed return better than most financial markets. Say you spend $3,000 on the energy-saving techniques listed here. If your yearly energy bill is $1,500, saving half of that will give you a return of $750, or 25 percent on your $3,000 outlay.

Better yet, if you borrow the $3,000 from your bank on a home-equity loan, you may spend the first five years paying it back out of the savings on your utility bill (sooner if you get a rebate from your utility). But after that, it's fat city. You'll be getting savings of $750 a year free and clear, without having to put up any money at all. This something-out-of-nothing return is a great illustration of what efficient energy use is all about. The savings you create become cash in the bank. Now *that's* investing!

An added bonus, if you need one, is that you will have reduced your home's contribution to pollution and greenhouse gases by one-half. Now, if we could convince everyone to do the same . . .

Office buildings are now being designed and built that use up to 75 percent less energy than existing buildings. These buildings have better lighting, heating and cooling, and space arrangements as well as more pleasant ambience—they are, in a word, "smarter" buildings. An added advantage is that these carefully crafted office spaces often raise the productivity of the office staff. In some businesses, a one percent rise in productivity can be even more cost-saving than the energy reduction.

INDUSTRIAL-STRENGTH SAVINGS

The 500 largest corporations in the world generate half of the air pollutants produced by world industry. This figure takes us back to chapter 2 and the importance of keeping pressure on these companies to adhere to ecological practices. While these firms are beginning to utilize some of the energy-saving practices mentioned in this chapter, the progress could be much faster.

Industrial workplaces and office buildings can make the same energy-saving changes as homes and pocket the money from lower utility bills. Industries that generate their own electricity can save even more by a process called cogeneration.

Cogeneration involves reclaiming waste heat. Using any fuel such as oil, coal, or natural gas to power an electric generator also produces a lot of heat. The internal combustion engine in your car, for example, needs a complicated cooling system to keep the engine from running too hot. In this case, most of the heat is just blown off into the atmosphere.

A small amount of the water used to cool the engine, however, is channeled into the heater of your car. This is cogeneration on a small scale—using the excess heat from an engine for space heating. Cogeneration on a large scale uses as much of the excess heat as possible from a fuel-powered electric generator to produce steam.

The steam is then used in other industrial processes or employed to heat buildings.

Using this heat essentially doubles the efficiency of an electric generator, allowing for efficiencies as high as 80 percent. This means half as much fuel burned and half as much pollution. Industrial cogeneration now amounts to about 30,000 megawatts in the U.S. In Paris and Stockholm, heat from cogeneration is used in large areas of the cities.

Some utilities in this country are also finding ways of using the wasted heat from their generators. Applied Energy Services, the Virginia utility profiled in chapter 2, builds cogeneration plants. One, in Uncasville, Connecticut, sells electricity to Connecticut Light and Power and steam to the Stone Container Corporation.

ELECTRIC MOTORS

Electric motors account for about half of the electricity used in most countries. Amory Lovins figures that about half of that power could be saved by smarter design and advanced motor technology. He speaks of improvements in the choice, sizing, and maintenance of the motors as well as their controls, electric supplies, and drivetrains.

Because about three-quarters of industrial electricity goes to run motors, increased efficiencies would result in tremendous savings.

ADDING IT UP

Increasing the efficiency of our energy use is the first and most important move toward a sustainable economy. Negawatts are by far the most cost-effective energy source, one which needs to be utilized to the fullest extent.

More efficient lighting, heating, and cooling, cogeneration, and improved electric motor design are the kinds of improvements that can save us 75 percent of our national electric bill. Better building design and home and commercial retrofits of insulation and weatherproofing will mean great reductions in oil and natural gas used for heating.

As we move toward more efficient vehicles, as described in chapter 9, we will effect another tremendous savings in our energy costs. These negabarrels of oil will save consumers money, reduce pollution, and almost eliminate our negative trade balance.

Bringing energy use way down will also aid in the introduction of renewable energy sources. Most estimates for switching to renewable sources assume consumption patterns similar to the present. In these projections, half of Arizona is covered with solar collectors, and all available wind sites across the country are filled with wind generators.

But a 75 percent reduction in electricity use would mean a 75 percent reduction in the number of photovoltaic panels, wind farms, and biomass generators needed to produce the power. This is 75 percent less investment capital and 75 percent less area needed for the production of power. With figures like these, an economy based on renewable energy suddenly seems much closer.

It bears repeating that increased efficiency does *not* have to mean reduced comfort or convenience. This is because smart technology gets more from less. Lowering energy use is a win-win-win-win situation all around: for consumers, utilities, industry, and our national economy.

COMPANIES

The companies which will take advantage of the energy-saving revolution will be those making and selling energy-saving products. Real Goods comes to mind right now, but watch as other public companies enter the arena.

CHAPTER 12

RAW MATERIALS

BACK TO THE FUTURE!

In the year 2050, most raw materials for industry come from recycled or renewable sources. Many materials, such as steel, have been largely replaced by composites made from renewable sources. The cultivation of trees and other plants is done in harmony with the ecosystems of which they are a part.

The extraction of unrenewable materials, such as metals, is done in a manner friendly to the ecology of the region. A flight over a copper mining area in northern Mexico reveals only a few mines. You don't see the worked-out mines because the landscapes around them have been returned to a natural state—as they will eventually be around the operating mines.

A visitor from the late twentieth century would be struck by the amount of forest cover. In every part of the world, forests are regrowing, along with their biodiverse ecosystems. Because the need for wood has been greatly

reduced, well-managed tree plantations along with se-
lected cutting in some established forests fulfill the
world's demand.

A pipe dream? Not at all. This future will come about
because of hard economic realities. The first of these realities is that, at our present rate of consumption, we will
run out of many raw materials in the twenty-first
century. We're simply not going to be able to conduct
business as usual in the realm of raw materials.

The second reality is that certain uses of many materials, such as wood, are wasteful and uneconomic. Paper, for example, which is presently made from wood
pulp, can be fabricated better and cheaper from other
materials, such as hemp. There many other instances of
misused raw materials.

The third economic reality is that there are new
materials—many from renewable sources—that do the
job better than the old, unrenewable ones. Remember
the ultralight vehicle described in chapter 9? Polymer
composites, as strong as steel and much lighter, will form
most of the chassis and body. There are new thermo-
plastic resins, called polysulfonic polymers, which are
presently being tested in Germany. These can be recycled
and reformed up to eighty times before seeing any
degeneration.

HITTING THE WALL

In the environmental realm, some problems that appear
temporarily better are actually getting worse. For example, over the last decade, the price of some raw materials,
such as metals, has dropped because extraction methods
have improved. That's good, isn't it? No, that's bad. While
the resulting increase in supplies may have lowered

prices, it has also brought the day closer when we run out of these materials.

These low prices are further encouraged by archaic government policies in this country that essentially give away mineral and timber rights on government lands. The mining and timber industries also benefit from generous tax exemptions. These policies, and others like them, were formulated in the nineteenth century to encourage the development of American industry. But efforts to revise them have been vigorously—and successfully—opposed by the large mining and lumber companies.

In chapter 1, we discussed the environmental organization, The Natural Step. The founder, Dr. Karl-Henrik Robert, speaks of certain industries "heading for a wall" because they are not considering basic environmental realities. In the case of many producers of raw materials, the wall is going to be a lack of supply.

To keep from hitting the wall, the largest "new" supply of all raw materials is going to have to come from recycling. As we discussed in chapter 6, industry programs have already begun in many countries to recycle most manufactured goods. Metals, plastics, paper, wood, glass, and virtually every other natural and fabricated material will be recycled in one form or another, and the savings in materials and energy will be enormous.

FORESTS FOREVER

It's difficult to find someone who doesn't like trees. Humans, after all, are supposedly descended from tree dwellers. After providing a habitat for our very early ancestors, trees provided shelter, tools, and eventually fuel for fires to our later forebears. Our entire evolution as a species has depended greatly on trees—our evolution, and that of a few hundred thousand other species.

Forests harbor a greater abundance of species than any other ecological zone. They are the major gene reservoirs of the planet and are the main sites where new life-forms emerge. The tropical rain forests alone contain at least 70 percent of all species on the planet.

Forests are a major part of the planetary recycling of carbon, nitrogen, and oxygen. They affect rainfall, climate, and temperature. They also build up fertile soil and prevent its erosion.

And, after a million years of human evolution, we still depend on forest products for much of our fuel and industry. Half the world's people still use wood for fuel; this accounts for about half the yearly consumption of wood, while industry uses the other half.

We will still need wood in the next century, though the amount we use will decrease tremendously. In all major areas of its use, wood will be mostly replaced by other more cost-effective materials. Other renewable sources of energy will partially replace wood as fuel; cheaper, more effective building materials will supplant lumber; and paper will be fabricated from faster-growing, more easily used plants.

A certain number of well-managed woodlands may still be necessary. These forests should be looked on more as cropland than as traditional forest areas, which are replete with diverse wildlife.

At the same time, the true forests will be regrowing all over the world. Sharply reducing the amount of wood used for fuel, construction, and paper making will free up so much area presently in tree plantations that traditional forests can be encouraged to grow on that land.

HEMP, THE TWENTY-FIRST CENTURY WONDER PLANT

Listen to the proponents of hemp, and you come away thinking that most of the material needs of the twenty-first century could be filled by this remarkable plant. Yes, hemp is what they make ropes out of; and yes, hemp is another name for cannabis, aka marijuana. But its backers swear that hemp has had a bad rap—that industrial hemp has never been psychoactive.

Hemp, in fact, has had a long and distinguished career in this country and abroad. Both George Washington and Thomas Jefferson grew hemp. The first two drafts of the Declaration of Independence were written on hemp paper. The Continental Army was outfitted in uniforms made from hemp linen.

Rope, paper, linen . . . this is only the beginning! How about construction materials such as composite paneling and fiberboard trusses and support beams? How about textiles of all different kinds? Animal feed? Human food? Or what about pharmaceuticals, plastics, and cosmetics?

To get a full picture of the many uses of this amazing plant, order the book, *Industrial Hemp* listed in *Resources*. As soon as hemp is legalized, investors should be on the lookout for a burgeoning industry.

WHY WRITE ON WOOD?

It's no mystery why wood began to be used as pulp for the manufacture of paper. Forests were plentiful. What is a mystery is why we persist in using wood pulp today when there are so many better alternatives. Paper can be made

Archaic Laws Prevent New Technology

In spite of its many uses, hemp fell victim to the anti-drug hysteria of the 1930s. Drug enforcement agents fomented public fears concerning marijuana. Because it resembled psychoactive marijuana, the cultivation of hemp was banned, and the drug agents harassed hemp manufacurers out of business.

This was a dismal chapter in American history, but the worst of it is that it's still with us. This is a prime example of how archaic laws, with the support of special interests, prevent improved technologies from moving us forward. Many industrial countries are beginning to produce large quantities of hemp and benefitting from its many uses while the U.S. is still stuck in the 1930s.

This is beginning to change. The governor of Kentucky has appointed a task force to look at the possibility of tobacco growers switching to hemp. And more than 200 firms now offer a wide variety of products made from hemp (importing hemp is legal). In this case, as well as in others, competition from other countries will probably be the motivating force for change. Legalization of hemp growing probably sometime before the turn of the century, is inevitable.

from a large number of plants, most of which grow faster than trees and produce more biomass per acre.

Hemp plants, for example, grow as high as six to 16 feet tall in 70 to 100 days and yield six to ten tons of fiber per acre. This makes the plant three to five times more productive than southern pine, which is often used as pulp for paper.

Hemp is as hardy as most weeds, it doesn't need pesticides, and it requires only a small amount of fertilizer (which can be organic). Making paper from hemp requires less energy and significantly fewer chemicals than making paper from wood pulp. This is especially important because paper making in its present form is a highly chemical-intensive process. Water pollution from paper mills, particularly the ubiquitous organochlorines, is a serious problem.

Paper made from hemp is superior to that made from wood. Hemp paper more than 1,500 years old has been found; not only does it resist decomposition, it doesn't turn yellow like old wood-based paper. And because of the strength of the hemp fiber, paper made from hemp can be recycled several times more than paper made from wood.

To add to these advantages, hemp is a cash crop that can be profitably grown by small farmers. And because paper production with hemp is relatively clean, small paper mills could be located in communities near the farms. This kind of small industry provides jobs and helps local economies.

SUSTAINABLE RAW MATERIALS

Hemp is one of the most promising, but many other raw materials can also be grown by small farms. Organically grown cotton is a growing source for natural clothing—so is wool spun from sheep raised without chemicals. Many nonfood crops can be cultivated in different areas of the U.S: jojoba for oil in the southwest, milkweed for down comforters in the northeast. Hemp can be grown in the midwest and the north; kenaf, a legal cousin of hemp, thrives in the south.

A sustainable economy can be more decentralized than our present system. More raw materials can be grown on small farms for local industries. We have grown accustomed to thinking big—big industry, big farms—but this concentration on size has resulted too often in the degradation of local economies.

Just as recycling has created many small local industries, the increased production of diverse raw materials will do the same.

COMPANIES

The Arizona Copper Company (AZCO) (AZC, AMEX) *800-563-7939*

While recycling can provide many of the raw materials we need, for the foreseeable future, we will still need virgin materials. Until we are able to build the kind of molecular replicators portrayed on *Star Trek,* we will need to cut trees, fabricate plastics, and mine metals.

We don't need to make a mess of things, however, as we have done up to now. The mining industry has been especially guilty of devastating the environment on a large scale. Situating a mine of any kind in a region has usually meant ecological disaster. Whole hillsides are ripped away, piles of discarded ore cover the ground, and chemicals used in the extraction process pollute the streams and groundwater. Some mining companies have made stabs at restoring landscapes, but most areas remain permanently scarred.

It doesn't have to be this way. A few companies are beginning to use new extraction techniques that do little damage to the surroundings. And, when the mine is played out, they are restoring the land to as close to its original state as possible.

The Arizona Copper Company (AZCO) is one such company. AZCO uses a technique called solvent extraction/electro winning. Because this extraction process takes place in self-contained tanks, there is little toxic discharge of chemicals into the surrounding area.

The process has further environmental advantages in that it allows for the extraction of copper from copper oxide ores. Up to now, these ores have been passed over because the traditional smelting process could only handle copper sulfide ores. What this means is that ores that were previously considered waste can be reprocessed. This is recycling, mining style.

When finished with a mine, AZCO stabilizes the waste rock dumps to prevent erosion, re-creates the topography of the land, and replants with native plants.

This kind of care is still, unfortunately, the exception in the world of mining. But it is presented here as an example of the way things ought to be. The solvent extraction technique now accounts for about 15 percent of the total supply of mined copper worldwide, and that number is continuing to rise.

* * *

Hemp is coming! And when it does, it's going to be big business. Watch first for Canadian companies that market hemp products. Because of our archaic laws concerning hemp, we may have to wait a few years to see hemp firms in the U.S., but they will come.

* * *

The paulownia tree is a "wonder tree" that has an amazing rate of growth, adapts to a wide range of climatic and soil conditions, enhances depleted and abused soils, and provides a superior hardwood. Because of these qualities, the paulownia has been touted as a solution to the erosion and depletion of forest resources in many developing countries.

There are several small public companies developing plantations of these trees, among them Forestry International (San Diego) and Saddle Mountain Timber Corporation (Vancouver). While these firms are still very much in the start-up phase, investors would do well to watch them closely. The paulownia could be an important boon to developing countries and an important source of lumber for the world.

Resources

Industrial Hemp: Practical Products—Paper to Fabric to Cosmetics (HEMPTECH, 1995 $4.95).

This 50-page booklet details the history and the many uses of hemp. It also describes the present progress towards legalization. To order, call HEMPTECH at 800-265-HEMP or 805-646-HEMP.

CHAPTER 13

THE CLEAN-UP CREW

"We Have Met the Enemy and He is Us."
—*POGO*

A STRUGGLE FOR SURVIVAL

In the summer of 1940, when Britain faced Nazi Germany alone, there was in that country not only a sense of solidarity, but a powerful sense of history. People speak of the awful anxiety of that time, but also of the pervasive feeling that they were involved in a struggle not just for their country, but for the survival of human freedom, even of civilization itself.

We are presently involved in a struggle that is no less momentous. It involves the survival of life as we know it, the future of our species and of others. This struggle, however, is not as clearly defined as wartime conflicts; even the identity of the enemy is often unclear. Too often, as Walt Kelly's Pogo points out, he bears an uncanny resemblance to us.

While everyone agrees that preserving the environment is important, exactly how to do this is a source of much contention. And, because this battle is measured in decades instead of months and years, who is winning is often very difficult to measure.

We have discussed many ways in which the ecosystem, our health, and our economy are threatened by old technologies, and how the new technologies can help. But no threats are more serious than those posed by the toxic substances in our air, water, and soil. It is these dangers in particular that make the struggle for our environment similar to a wartime struggle for survival.

THE ORGANOCHLORINES

Take organochlorines, for example. Organochlorines are injuring our health and, perhaps, killing us, but they are doing it so slowly that much of the damage is invisible. Many of these compounds are already infamous: DDT, for one, or dioxins, PCBs, and CFCs.

Organochlorines find their way into the environment from a long list of different sources. Dioxins are released from incinerating wastes or from the chlorine bleaches used in the production of paper. Pesticides and fungicides put these chemicals into the air and soil and industrial processes add many more.

These compounds are everywhere—in the soil where our food grows, in the water we drink, and in the air we breathe. Because they do not break down easily, they accumulate in all organisms, but especially in the fatty tissues of those at the top of the food chain, like humans.

The organochlorines, besides causing cancer, birth defects, and suppression of the immune system, are also beginning to be implicated in infertility. In every country in the world, the quantity and density of men's sperm has been declining, often by as much as half. Although researchers are not yet certain, they suspect the organochlorines because they tend to disrupt the endocrine system of the body.

There is no doubt as to the toxicity of these and other chemicals, heavy metals, and radioactive materials that we dump into the ecosystem. But scientists often have a difficult time ascertaining just which of these substances now present in the environment—and in what quantities—cause health problems in humans and other animals. This is because there are so many unnatural compounds out there, and the damage they do can occur over years and sometimes decades. All researchers can do is watch "cancer clusters" appear near certain industries or toxic waste dumps and catalog the occurrence of other illnesses that seem to be chemically caused.

This is the kind of struggle we're involved in: industry doesn't want to stop producing and disposing of organochlorines or other life-damaging chemicals because there is no "hard" proof that they are harmful in the relatively small quantities present in the environment. And the hard proof may not be available for decades, by which time the damage will almost certainly be much worse. This is a bad catch-22 situation because there are many, many toxic substances like the organochlorines being put out into the ecosystem.

CLEANING UP

Women sometimes say that one reason the environment is in such a mess is that men are not used to cleaning up after themselves. There certainly has been an attitude among those in power (who have indeed been mostly men) that the consequences of throwing toxic substances into the environment were not something they needed to worry about.

We are now paying for that cavalier attitude. The Environmental Protection Agency (EPA) estimates that it will cost $60 billion to clean up the 2,400 most contaminated sites on its Superfund priority list. There are potentially 90,000 of these sites. This is money which is not going to pay off the national debt, not going to build schools or roads or to care for the sick.

If this was the end of it—if no more toxics were being produced—it would still be a very dangerous, expensive situation. But hazardous substances are still being disposed of in irresponsible ways. According to the EPA, 22 billion pounds of toxic chemicals are released into the air, water, and soil by American industry each year. This means there will be more toxic sites in the future, which we will have to spend money on to clean up. Potential ecological damage aside, this is obviously terrible economics.

THE PROBLEMS

In other chapters, we have already discussed many of the problems associated with hazardous substances in the environment and looked at some solutions. For example, recycling many of these substances keeps them from being disposed of in landfills. Changing to organic agriculture eliminates the use of chemicals to grow our food. And, of course, using less energy and employing renewable energy means a reduction in air pollution from the burning of fossil fuels.

But what about the stuff that's already in the soil and water? What do we do with that? And what about the waste that continues to pour into the ecosystem? Let's look at the areas where these problems are; then in the next section we'll talk about solutions.

Toxic Materials in Groundwater Groundwater, which is often used for drinking water, is contaminated by metals such as lead, mercury, cadmium, and arsenic as well as asbestos, the ubiquitous organochlorines, and other chemicals.

Buried Waste Many hazardous materials, especially petro-chemicals, have been buried in unlined fills or in tanks that corrode over time. The waste then filters into the groundwater and/or pollutes the surrounding soil, making the area unusable and often dangerous to health.

Radioactive Waste The Department of Energy estimates that by the year 2000, 50,000 metric tons of spent fuel will have accumulated at nuclear power plant sites. The term "spent," is misleading; this is fuel that has become too radioactive to use! In addition, 200,000 cubic feet of radioactive waste is produced each year by nuclear weapons manufacturing. The Office of Technology Assessment says that "air, water sediments, soil, vegetation, and wildlife" have been badly contaminated at these weapons sites.

Man-made Lagoons There are roughly 180,000 man-made lagoons, at municipal and industrial sites, which have been used for the disposal of various types of wastes, many of them toxic. Most of these are unlined, and many are near water supplies. What is actually in these lagoons is not well-known.

Oil Spills Oil continues to be spilled into ocean and bay waters from tanker accidents. Oil is also spilled on land, polluting the soil and groundwater.

Ocean Pollution Most pollutants eventually find their way to the ocean, where many of them are ingested by marine creatures. The heavy metals that contaminate

groundwater are also found in the fish we eat, organochlorines pollute many areas, and there are increasing
die-offs of marine mammals.

NONSOLUTIONS

Many solutions have been tried for this enormous problem of toxic wastes. Some are successful, some not so
good, and some seem to cause more problems than they
solve. There are a large number of firms that deal with
various forms of disposal and detoxification; because of
the quantity and variety of these methods, it's important
for investors to know which of these technologies is truly
environmentally friendly.

To begin with, let's look at a few waste treatment
methods that *don't* work, either in economic or environmental terms.

First among these is incineration. All the problems
we mentioned in chapter 7 concerning the incineration of
household garbage are doubly true about the burning of
hazardous waste. This is a nonsolution: the smoke is poisonous, the smokestack scrubbers trap only a portion of
it, and the toxicity is concentrated in the ash.

There are a few methods being researched that use
high-temperature thermal processes to destroy certain
types of hazardous substances. While heat is part of
these processes, the end results are much less toxic than
those from incineration.

The most promising of these experimental methods
is a project carried on at the University of Dayton,
under the sponsorship of the National Renewable Energy
Laboratory. Called the "High-Temperature Photochemi-
cal Destruction of Toxic Organic Waste Using Concentrated Solar Radiation," this process breaks down and

destroys certain organic compounds with concentrated sunlight. More research needs to be done, but this is one of those promising technologies to watch.

The practice of burying hazardous waste is another nonsolution. This method works on the "out of sight, out of mind" theory. But the toxics are only gone for as long as it takes for their containers or plastic liners to degrade; then the chemicals start showing up—Surprise!—in the soil, the groundwater, and the food chain.

In fact, digging up and disposing of deteriorating storage tanks is one of the primary businesses of waste management companies. How these companies then handle the tanks and their contents varies greatly; investors need to research this before investing in a supposedly environmentally concerned waste disposal firm.

Burying is, unfortunately, the preferred method for the disposal of nuclear wastes; in fact, after hundreds of billions of dollars of research, this is virtually the *only* solution they've come up with. We are asked to be extremely optimistic that these incredibly radioactive substances can be buried in tanks, natural caves, or man-made caverns and will not be disturbed for the hundreds of thousands of years it takes for them to lose their radioactivity.

This is asking a great deal of optimism, particularly given the shaky, obfuscating record of those in charge of disposing of nuclear materials. At the nuclear weapons plant in Hanford, Washington, almost a million gallons of radioactive waste has escaped from containment tanks since 1958 and contaminated the water table. The Department of Energy has only recently admitted that hundreds of thousands of people living near weapons plants in other states have been exposed to radioactive releases since 1945.

The clean-up and disposal of nuclear wastes is a problem that won't go away anytime soon. But the nuclear industry still argues for nuclear power, and the government still is producing—and testing—nuclear weapons.

There is not the space to pursue this subject further in this book. The horror stories about releases, leaking storage tanks, and cancers and birth defects are repeated almost everywhere in the world. But if you understand simply that the use, shipping, and storage of nuclear materials are activities fraught with danger and the possibilities of terrible accidents, you know much of what you need to about the subject.

At present, there is simply no good way to store the massive amounts of radioactive waste that have been—and are still being—produced. We should view the underground storage presently being employed as a temporary solution, not a permanent one. If future research discovers a better way to deal with this waste, we need to use it on these buried time bombs. Earthquakes, volcanic activity, terrorists, civil unrest—any of these could easily spread this life-destroying radiation. We simply cannot leave this venomous legacy to our children and grandchildren.

REAL SOLUTIONS

Simply throwing away hazardous waste doesn't work because nature doesn't know how to break it down and recycle it. It just builds up in the ecosystem causing myriad problems, some of which we are already aware of, others of which we only suspect. Incinerating it with present technology leaves us with even more concentrated toxics to dispose of. And burying it in tanks or landfills simply shifts the period of pollution from the present to the future.

There are, however, beginning to be real solutions to at least some of the problems of toxic clean-up and disposal. This is an area that has only begun to be seriously researched during the last two decades. The innovative technology that has already appeared is a hopeful sign, even though much more research needs to be done.

Pollution that has found its way into the ground doesn't go away easily. Toxic material buried in the earth can make certain areas unliveable and unusable for any purpose. In addition, the toxins often leach into the groundwater, poisoning water supplies for agriculture and human consumption.

The most common remedy for soil polluted with chemicals or petroleum is to dig it up and incinerate it. In addition to the drawbacks of incineration, however, this method often treats only the top layers of pollution. There is a much more environmentally friendly solution that can be used for many pollutants: this solution is called *bioremediation*.

Bioremediation is the method that the natural world has been using for millions of years. A leaf falling to the ground becomes a food source for microorganisms; as they eat the leaf, these microbes produce carbon dioxide and return beneficial nutrients to the soil. There are thousands of different kinds of microbes in the ground, with tastes for different organic substances. But they can also be encouraged to mutate so that they destroy unnatural substances, like chemical compounds.

In the early 1980s, an underground storage tank at a gas station in North Babylon, New York, leaked 30,000 gallons of gasoline into the soil. Some of this gas found its way to the water table and dispersed further. Nearby residents began to notice gasoline fumes in the basements of their homes.

Bioremediation engineers circulated air through the soil by means of vacuum pumps and then pumped oxygen and nutrients into the groundwater. The added oxygen and nutrients caused an explosion in the native population of soil microbes, which were already adapting to a diet of gasoline (Yum!). After eight years, almost all the gasoline had been removed from the soil.

This sounds relatively simply, but it's not. A different strategy for each site must be devised. For example, if the soil is too rocky or nonporous, like clay, the nutrients won't get to the microbes. Oxygen and nutrients must be carefully formulated to encourage the growth of microbe populations. And certain toxics do not easily lend themselves to this kind of treatment.

Unfortunately, salespeople for some bioremediation companies have touted the technology as a cure-all, and the industry has been damaged by these false claims as well as by a few disastrous failures from badly planned operations.

Nevertheless, this is the technology that shows the most promise for cleaning up polluted soil in an environmentally friendly manner. The microbes are like miniature chemical laboratories, converting some of the most complex—and toxic—molecules into simple carbon dioxide. And after the pollutant is all gone, the microbes revert to their normal diet of natural substances.

Up to now, bioremediation has achieved its greatest successes with petroleum-based spills. But researchers are now discovering and breeding microorganisms that will eat various kinds of exotic chemicals such as trichlorophenol, one of the two active ingredients in Agent Orange. This deadly herbicide, of Vietnam War infamy, was previously thought to be nonbiodegradable. A microbe population has also been discovered that will digest the toxic organochlorine, PCB.

Bioremediation is environmental technology at its best. The most successful solutions form *partnerships* with the natural world. Here we have nature's own clean-up crew, perfected over hundreds of millions of years; all we do is encourage these microbes to alter their diet and provide a rich environment for them to grow in.

Bioremediation techniques, like most environmental solutions, are usually cheaper than incineration or other methods. As this technology is perfected, it could be the answer to many of our most toxic clean-up problems. For example, experimental evidence is encouraging that bioremediation may work on oil spills in water. Investors should watch for companies at the cutting edge of this field.

THE ONLY REAL SOLUTION

The best solution to the problem of toxics in the environment, of course, is not to put them there in the first place. Since 1970, in the U.S. alone, we have spent about one trillion dollars to prevent and clean up all different kinds of waste and pollution. While some success has been achieved, this enormous amount of money has not come anywhere near to solving the problems. As any parent of small children can tell you, it's hard to clean up when more messes are constantly being made.

Industry argues that the products that cause the pollution are useful and necessary, and that the damage they cause has not been proved or quantified. Dr. Karl-Henrik Robert of The Natural Step (*Resources*, chapter 1) counters these arguments with six questions about the nature of any toxic which finds its way into the environment. In the case of most toxics, the answers run like this:

1. Is this substance natural?	No.
2. Is it stable?	Yes.
3. Does it degrade into harmless substances?	No.
4. Does it accumulate in bodily tissues?	Yes.
5. Can we predict acceptable tolerances?	No.
6. Can we continue to place this chemical in the environment?	No.

Dr. Robert's fifth question about acceptable tolerances is the key one here. We need to know just as much about any chemical that is released into the environment as we know about the drugs we ingest as medicines. If we can't predict the acceptable tolerances that our bodies can handle, how do we know that the substance is safe?

Any new pharmaceutical drug is subjected to years of the most intensive scrutiny. The criteria used by the Food and Drug Administration (FDA) is essentially "Guilty until proven innocent." In the case of environmental chemicals, however, the reverse has been the standard operating procedure. Even when it is proven that a given toxic released into the environment tends to build up in animal and human tissues, the chemical is "innocent" until the most stringent experiments have proved that it makes people sick.

If the FDA used this kind of criteria, there would be thousands of unproved, dangerous drugs on the market. And these drugs would be withdrawn not when people began to get sick, but only when years of scientific studies proved beyond a shadow of a doubt that they were, indeed, causing disease.

The chemical companies need to stop using us and other animals as the proving ground for the toxicity of the chemicals that are placed into the environment. They need to begin the shift to more benign substances while phasing out the toxics. This is the only real solution that will work in the long term.

As our technology improves, we can probably clean up the hazardous stuff already in the ecosystem. Natural processes will restore the balance in some cases; for example, the ozone layer appears to be healing itself as the release of CFCs into the atmosphere has decreased. The ocean waters seem to be able to clean themselves over time. But neither we nor nature can do it if the pollution continues. If we don't stop polluting, we will be overwhelmed with waste. In fact, we are approaching that point now.

LONG-TERM PARKING

Let's face it: there are quite a few hazardous substances that we simply don't know how to deal with. They can't be recycled or chemically broken down, and they can't be released into the environment. Burying them or incinerating them are nonsolutions because they don't really get rid of the toxics. Future technology may find ways to detoxify these substances, but in the meantime, they need to be stored.

So where shall we store them? Justus Englefried and Dr. Michael Braungart, of the Environmental Protection Encouragement Agency in Germany, propose that we create aboveground parking lots for these wastes. The lots would be owned by the state, but leased to the companies responsible for producing and using the chemicals.

This concept is similar to the cradle-go-grave recycling of products discussed in chapter 6 in that the manufacturer would be responsible for the final disposition of its products. Paul Hawken suggests that certain polluting chemicals could be molecularly tagged so that their producer could be easily found when the substances appear in the environment.

The beauty of this suggestion is that, because of the costs of recovering the substances and storing them indefinitely, the chemical companies would have a real incentive to start producing less toxic substances. Chemicals that can be reused, recycled, or biodegraded would be much more likely to arrive at the marketplace. And we might also see more research into ways of dealing with the waste compounds in the parking lots.

COMPANIES

There are many companies involved in environmental clean-up operations. Unfortunately, many of them use methods that are not environmentally sound. Investors need to investigate carefully to determine if their capital is supporting a real solution to a problem or is creating new problems.

A general rule is that firms that attempt to deal with waste by burying it, incinerating it, or simply carting it somewhere else are not considered environmental investments. Firms that use bioremediation and recycling techniques are very attractive, but the specific technologies they use need to be looked at carefully.

In the next few years, some chemical companies may decide to move toward producing more benign substances. If the move seems real and sincere, investors may want to encourage these firms by buying their stock, even if the product line is not yet all "green." The company has to look good financially, of course, but this is a case where the *direction* of a company should be carefully considered. Changes like these are not going to happen overnight, but incremental change should be applauded.

Global Spill Management, Inc.
(GSMI, NASDAQ) 610-631-5500

GSMI has been busy acquiring various firms with different waste management capabilities. The company can now provide services such as: emergency spill response and recovery (as in oil spills), tank removal and disposal, liquid and solid waste transportation and disposal, soil remediation, tank cleaning, and pipe rehabilitation.

As we have seen, it's becoming possible to clean up soil contaminated with petroleum products and some chemicals. Often, however, it's necessary to remove the underground tanks that are the source of the pollution. It's estimated that 750,000 underground storage tanks may need to be removed. This is a niche in the clean-up market that GSMI has positioned itself for.

In addition, the company has cleaned up large oil spills. Because tankers will, unfortunately, continue to have accidents, GSMI will also have a significant source of revenue from this part of its business.

Revenues have been growing fast at GSMI, and right now, the company looks very promising for investors. Be sure to get the latest information, however. Some acquisitive small firms have grown too fast and had to retrench.

Molten Metal Technology, Inc. (MLTN) *(MLTN, NASDAQ) 617-487-9700)*

Molten Metal Technology owns a patented process which reduces certain hazardous materials to basic chemical elements and gases. This Catalytic Extraction Process (CEP) employs molten metal heated to 3,000°F, with solvents used as catalysts. This is a closed system, so that any gases emitted are trapped and saved for recycling. The CEP process can handle waste products as diverse as PCBs and scrap circuit boards. Circuit boards are rich in gold, copper, iron, and nickel, which are recycled.

A related process called Quantum CEP even processes low-level radioactive waste. The waste is reduced in volume by a factor of 30 to 1, and stabilized for safe handling. The process is not perfect—waste still needs to be stored—but the volume is greatly reduced.

MLTN is expanding rapidly. The company has already established a reputation for dealing with toxic substances in a safe, environmentally-friendly manner. MLTN has made contracts with such giants as Lockheed

Martin and Westinghouse to build plants using the CEP process.

The company was started in 1989 and went public in February 1993. Revenues have been rising steadily at MLTN and 1996 may see positive earnings per share. This is extraordinary growth for a start-up company, and it confirms our belief that workable, environmentally-friendly technology is a rapid-growth industry.

CHAPTER 14

THE ECOLOGY OF INVESTING

Investors are sometimes frustrated in finding suitable companies in certain environmental areas. Some are too big. For example, in the field of renewable energy production, many of the players are large utilities. The renewable part of their power production still makes up such a small percentage of their total that they can hardly be classed as environmental. Indeed, many still own nuclear plants.

On the other end of the scale are thousands of companies working on the environment that are too small even to think about issuing stock. And many owners, even when their firms grow larger, simply choose to keep them privately owned.

Nevertheless, there is an ever-growing number of small publicly owned environmental companies, many of which are prime candidates for investment. The newsletters listed in *Resources* will show you how to find most of these companies.

As the entire environmental sector expands, many small companies will be formed to supply the larger ones. This has already begun in the renewable energy sphere; there are several independent power producers that sell wind- and solar-generated electricity to large utilities. Watch for more of these.

Keep a watch out also for firms selling renewable energy equipment to industry and government, such as Photocomm (see Solar Companies, chapter 4). There are bound to be more suppliers like this, and there will also be more firms selling to the public, such as Real Goods (chapter 10).

In the case of some of the brand-new, innovative technologies portrayed in this book, your best bet is simply to keep abreast of the latest developments. As you continue your research in the fields that most attract your interest, you will get a feeling for which technologies look most promising. And this will direct you to the firms that are working on them.

SMALL COMPANY STOCKS

In the field of the environment, you will find yourself looking mostly at small companies. Investing in small companies requires different strategies than investing in large companies or mutual funds because you are dealing with a much more volatile sector. We're going to look at how you can deal with this volatility and make your investments in small firms as safe as they are profitable.

Smallness has its advantages and drawbacks. On the plus side, small companies usually have a limited number of shares of stock. This means that should the company prosper, there will be investors clamoring for a small number of shares. The law of supply and demand will then drive the price of the stock up sharply.

In addition, small company stocks are usually priced very cheaply. This allows an individual investor to purchase a relatively large number of shares, which increases his or her potential for profit. For example, with $4,000, ignoring commissions, you could buy 2,000 shares of a $2 stock. The same amount of money would get you 100 shares of a $40 stock. If the $2 stock goes up in value by just $1, you will realize a $2,000 gain. The $40 stock would have to go up by 20 points to $60 to equal that gain—a much more unlikely possibility.

These are the built-in advantages to small companies. The built-in disadvantages are that because of their size, small firms are very sensitive to economic downturns, either in the whole economy or in their specific sector. A one-product business—which most small companies are—is going to have big trouble if the demand for its product falls off, even for a short time. Being lean and hungry may be good for getting ahead, but it also means you don't have any fat to live off of in hard times.

INVESTING SAFELY

So how can you, as an individual investor in small company stocks, cash in on the advantages of small companies while protecting yourself against the risks? For answers, let's compare mutual funds with small stock investments.

Two reasons that mutual funds are relatively secure investments are their diversity and professional management. A fund which holds stocks in fifty small companies is a safer investment than the stock of one small company; if a few of them have difficulties, you've got forty more to balance them. If the economy goes south, the fund may fall in value, but it will almost certainly stay alive to rise again when the economy turns around.

So, in order to safeguard your capital in small companies, you want to emulate the mutuals in certain ways. First, you want to diversify your holdings. Holding stock in only one or two small firms is a real recipe for disaster. You need to buy at least nine or ten companies—and they need to be in different fields. If you're buying environmental stocks, don't buy ten in waste management, even if that area looks terrific. Spread yourself around and you will benefit from the balance and diversity.

When you own a mutual fund, you pay a yearly fee for the professional management of your capital. What you're paying for mostly is the time spent by the managers in researching and choosing the best companies for the fund. If you choose your own companies, you're going to need to spend some of your own research time.

This time is what separates the real investors from the gamblers. The great majority of small investors buy stocks on the scantiest amount of information. "Uncle Joe says . . ." or "Jim, down at work, says . . ." Buying stocks in this manner is much closer to gambling than to investing. By doing some real research, you are taking yourself out of the company of gamblers and placing yourself in a category much closer to the professional investor.

So, call up the company you're interested in. Get their investor's packet, read it and then call up the investor relations person with your questions. Get the professional analysts on your side by subscribing to a few investment newsletters. And take your time. Your safety here depends not on your speed, but on your deliberate slowness.

In the environmental field, this book is your first research tool. If you're new to investing or want to know more about the ins and outs of small company stocks, my two previous books, *Big Profits from Small Stocks,* and the *First Book of Investing,* will help get you started. And you will also find valuable tools in the form of newsletters listed in *Resources.*

Investing safely in small companies requires that they be only one part of a larger portfolio. This portfolio should ideally include blue chip stocks, top-rated bonds, international stocks, utility stocks, and some cash, as well as small companies. These different kinds of investments will give you the kind of balance you need to weather all kinds of economic storms. When one sector is down, other sectors may be up.

As a general rule, most investors should have a maximum of 20 percent of their capital in small company stocks. This will provide plenty of opportunities for growth, but will protect against temporary downturns in the economy or in the areas where your small caps are.

This diversification can be in the form of individual companies or mutual funds. If you choose your own individual stocks and bonds, you should be prepared to do plenty of research. Mutual funds are preferred by many investors because of their professional management. To find socially responsible companies or mutual funds, check *Resources* in chapter 2.

In the case of small companies, I'm assuming that most readers of this book will want to buy individual environmental companies. *Resources* in this chapter will direct you to the best places to find these firms. By now, you should know the basics of environmental technology, but be sure to research each firm carefully before putting any money down.

This research is especially important with small companies because you should expect to hold on to these stocks for several years. Safe small company investing means employing a buy-and-hold strategy. Be assured that you're in good company; such famous investors as Warren Buffett and Peter Lynch use the buy-and-hold method. They also favor plenty of research.

Let's summarize. To invest safely in small, environmental companies, you need:

1. Diversification. Buy a number of stocks in different fields.

2. Knowledge. You need to know as much as possible about any company before you invest.

3. Balance. Make sure your portfolio includes many different kinds of investments.

4. Patience. Small companies have proven to be the best investments of the twentieth century—*over time*. But they are constantly going up and down; to ensure that yours go up, you should expect to hold on to them for at least several years. Constantly trading the stock of small firms is closer to gambling than to investing.

Resources

Resources in chapter 2 includes several excellent newsletters that will help you choose investments in the larger field of socially responsible investments. The newsletters here deal specifically with companies in the environmental area.

New Energy Report. Bimonthly. $60.00/year. 84 Canyon Road, Fairfax, CA 94930, 415-459-2383.

The *New Energy Report* covers one company in depth in each issue. Firms are profiled from all the different environmental areas: solar, wind, recycling, marketing, organic food, and more. These are generally small companies; subscribers are urged to buy them and hold while they grow and their stock appreciates. Recently, the *New Energy Report* has incorporated a stock trading portfolio that covers other areas of SRI as well as environmental. The editor is Samuel Case (the author of this book).

The Environmental Investor's Newsletter. Six issues. $59.00/year. Chasen & Luck Communications, 410 North Bronson Avenue, Los Angeles, CA 90004-1504. 800-995-1903.

To find the many environmental companies in this country and Canada, this is the newsletter you want. Started in

1990, *The Environmental Investor's Newsletter* has published more than 250 corporate profiles. No recommendations are made—you're strictly on your own. If a company sounds interesting, you need to call them up and ask for their investor's packet.

Chasen & Luck have several other SRI publications, including *The Environmental Investor's Directory of Socially Responsible Public Companies.* This includes brief profiles of more than 400 companies you can buy stock in ($120. Same address).

You can also join their Environmental Investor's Network and receive information (brochures, press releases, annual reports, etc.) directly from environmental firms in any sector you designate. Contact Chasen & Luck for this and additional services and publications.

CHAPTER 15

BUILDING FOR THE FUTURE

MAINTAINING A BALANCE

A friend of mine had just started seeing a psychotherapist, but was already despairing of making any real changes. "The aspects of me which are used to the status quo are like this big brass band, marching in lockstep," he moaned, "and the part of me that wants to change is like this little, lone flute player trying to make himself heard over the band."

We live in a time of death and new birth: many of the the old ways are dying, but they're not going out gracefully because so many people feel threatened by the changes. The new ways are already here or are in the research laboratories, but spreading the word is often difficult. The brass bands of the status quo often seem to have a corner on the power and money necessary to effect real change.

In the face of these vested interests and the massive degradation of the environment presently occurring, many people tend to lose heart. Despair is an occupational hazard of those in the environmental movement.

While we need to be aware of the difficulties, there is nevertheless much to be hopeful about. I see the new, sustainable technology portrayed in this book as essentially making an end run around the powers that be. These technologies are beginning to succeed all over the world, sometimes with the help of government and big business, sometimes not. Costs are falling, efficiencies are rising, and new research is burgeoning.

And in legislative offices and corporate boardrooms, people in power are beginning to listen to the environmental thinkers and planners. The language of the twenty-first century is starting to be heard.

INVESTING IN THE ENVIRONMENT

This book is about investing. But the subject can be broadened to include placing capital in more immediate places, such as energy-efficient products for the home. As we saw in chapter 11, the money saved from reduced utility bills provides an excellent return on investment. Buying a more efficient vehicle will also save you money on fuel.

Immediate monetary returns aside, supporting the environment in every way possible is an investment in the future—the future of the human race and of the other species who share our planet with us. Time spent in separating recyclables, helping your community clean up a polluted area, or writing your Congressperson on a bill affecting the environment is an investment. Sometimes the payoff is immediate, sometimes years away.

The return from some of these investments can't be measured in money. A society more in tune with the environment is simply a healthier, more pleasant place to live. But such a society is also likely to have a more prosperous economy. Technology that takes ecological systems into account is better technology: it's more efficient and, therefore, cheaper; it's nonpolluting, sustainable, and helps create jobs in local economies.

Our vision of the year 2050, while optimistic, is also realistically obtainable; most of the technology to make it happen is already here. Sustainable technology is, as we have seen, optimistic by nature because it empowers people and sustains life.

If this is true, then employing practices that restore and sustain the environment should also change our emotional lives. Because we are part of our environment, using technology that harmonizes with natural rhythms in the ecosystem will also help us to feel more in tune.

Then, all we would need to bring about our vision of 2050 would be for all of us to view each other as important parts of the environment to be nurtured and sustained. This is the final step that will allow us to move toward the creation of the kind of society we have only dreamed about.

Resources

Ecopsychology: Restoring the Earth, Healing the Mind, edited by Theodore Roszak, Mary E. Gomes, and Allen D. Kanner (Sierra Club Books, 1995).

The theme of this fine collection of essays, as Lester Brown writes in the Foreword, is that . . . *the human psyche [is] an integral part of the web of nature.* Twenty-six psychologists and ecologists explore the concept that our mental health may be connected to the health of the planet. If this is true, then ecological degradation must affect us all, and the despair and depression experienced by so many people must come from more than just individual difficulties.

Why is this pertinent to what we have been discussing in this book? Because the manner in which traditional psychotherapy has separated the individual psyche from what goes on in the world is similar to the way technology has been separated from its effects on the environment. As we promote sustainable technology that is harmonious with the Earth's natural systems, we are affirming that we too are part of the great, interconnected web of life. And this affirmation will help us to heal and reintegrate ourselves and our society.

SOCIALLY RESPONSIBLE MUTUAL FUNDS

L ike other mutual funds, the performance of the socially responsible (SR) funds depends entirely on the skill of the managers. There is a great deal of variability among these funds. Call the 800 number for a prospectus and check out the performance over the last five years. There is no reason for SR investors to settle for anything less than top returns.

The funds listed here are true SR funds. As we discussed in chapter 2, there are various funds which call themselves "environmental" but invest in some of the biggest polluters.

Growth funds will generally show higher returns than balanced funds. This is because the growth funds are generally riskier than the balanced. Fund performance should be compared with others in the same category.

For updates on SR mutual funds, join Co-op America (*Resources*, chapter 2) and ask for their booklet *You, Your Money and the World*. They include SR ratings for each fund—the negative and positive screens used to pick the companies in their portfolios (screens are explained in chapter 2).

Here are some of the best-performing SR funds:

Growth Stock Funds

As a group, the SR growth funds have had a very uneven record over the past five years. Two growth funds, however, have outstanding records: the Parnassus Fund over the last ten years and the Bridgeway Fund for the first-year-and-a-half of its existence.

The Parnassus Fund   This aggressive growth fund selects out-of-favor, undervalued companies. Its returns over the last five years place it among the top performers of *all* growth funds, SR or not.

There is a load (initial fee) of 3.5 percent and a minimum initial investment of $2,000. Call for the most recent figures and a prospectus.

800-999-3505.

The Bridgeway Fund   Started in August 1994, Bridgeway has three portfolios: The Ultra-Small Company Portfolio, the Aggressive Growth Portfolio, and The Social Responsibility Portfolio. Investors can specify which one they want. If you join, you will be sent a questionnaire asking which categories of SRI you would like the managers to emphasize (environmental, minority advancement, community outreach, etc.). This is a feature that the other SR funds would do well to emulate.

The performance of all three Bridgway portfolios has been excellent from the beginning. This is a no-load fund. Minimum initial investment is $2,000.

800-661-3550.

Balanced Funds

Balanced funds own a mix of stocks and fixed income investments (such as bonds). Because of the relative stability of the fixed-income assets, the funds are less volatile than the stock growth funds.

Pax World Fund   The oldest (1971) of the socially screened funds, PAX has traditionally shown excellent returns. A couple of low-performing years in the early 1990s had investors worried, but a fine return in 1995 put the fund back on track.

This is a no-load fund, with an initial requirement of only $250, making PAX perfect for low-income investors.

800-767-1729.

Calvert Social Managed Growth   Another fine SR balanced fund, Calvert has had a good record over the last ten years and showed an excellent performance in 1995.

There is a 4.75 percent load to buy this fund and a $1,000 minimum initial investment.

800-368-2748.

DEVCAP Shared Return Fund

Here's an interesting concept for a mutual fund. At the end of each year, you can choose to donate half or more of your return from this fund to four leading not-for-profit organizations with worldwide concerns. DEVCAP is, in fact, a consortium of these organizations: Save the Children, Seed Capital Development Fund, Catholic Relief Services, and Appropriate Technology International.

These four organizations have a special interest in micro-lending programs, which lend small amounts of seed capital to would-be entrepreneurs throughout the developing world. The amounts of these loans are indeed micro, often no more than $50–$100, but they might allow a farmer to buy a few pigs and work his way out of poverty, or enable a group of women to buy a loom and start a weaving cooperative. The repayment rate on these loans has run close to 100% and the repaid money is recycled to other microentrepreneurs.

These are exciting programs—they have already helped thousands of people lift themselves out of poverty, and the movement is growing. DEVCAP was formed in 1992 to channel the resources of the American financial world to the villages of the developing world (for DEV-CAP, *Development Capital*). Your contribution is tax-deductible.

DEVCAP is what is known as an index fund. Instead of following the S&P 500, however, it invests in the companies of the Domini Social Index. This index consists of stocks from 400 U.S. companies chosen for their corporate and social responsibility, as well as their financial performance. Since its inception in 1990, the Domini Index has consistently outperformed the S&P 500 Index.

DEVCAP is a no-loan fund. Minimum initial investment is $1,000.

800-371-2655

INDEX

Organochlorines (DDT, PCBs, CFCs)
effects of, 4, 156
microbe population to digest, 164
sources of, 156
Oxfam America, 27
Ozone layer, healing of, 166

P

Pacific Gas & Electric, 137
Paper production
misuse of wood for, 146, 149–50
from recycled paper, 82–83
in 2050 C.E., 82
Parnassus Fund, The, 184
Paulownia trees, 153–54
Pax World Fund, 185
Personal rail car, 124–25
Pesticides
alternatives to using, 102
countries banning, 100
disappearance of chemical, 95
effects on children of, 98
growing immunity of pests to, 99
nonspecificity of, 97
used in developing nations, 4, 96
Petroleum
cleaning up soil contaminated
with, 168–69
importing, 106–7
inefficiency of using, 9, 107
political problems with, 107
spills of, 159
U.S. and world use of, 71
Photocomm, Inc., 53–54, 74–75
Photovoltaic cells
companies manufacturing, 54
as complement to wind power in
hybrid systems, 60
costs of, 41, 45–46, 72–73
efficiency of, 44–45
invention of, 40
lack of commercial development
of, 41
Photovoltaic material
for large buildings, 42
on roofs, 39, 42
Photovoltaic power
to charge car battery pack, 123
costs of, 72–73

distribution of, 48
storage of, 46–48
Plants as a fuel source, 66–70
Polysulfonic polymers, 146
Population
poverty, sustainable technology,
and, 35–37
problem of, 36, 96
Positive screening of companies,
21–22
Poverty
environmental technology for
breaking out of cycle of, 37–38
population, and sustainable
technology, 35–37
Power plants, 40
Power storage for solar energy,
46–48
Predictions of the future, 1–16
Product recycling, 84–86
Progressive Asset Management
(PAM), 103
PV collector, 44

Q

Quality of life, raising efficiency of
technology to improve, 138
Quantum CEP, 169

R

Radioactive materials, 159
escaping from containment tanks
in Hanford, Washington, 161
toxicity of, 157
Raw materials, 145–54
companies for, 152–54
future sources of, 145
resources on, 154
savings from cutting back use of,
135–44
sustainable, 151–52
Real Goods Trading Company, 74,
130–34, 144
activities of, 131
"Eco-Audit" of, 131
as an environmental family,
132–33
Institute for Solar Living of, 133
sales of, 130

/